Shakespeare's Universality

For Roy
with every
good wish!
Kieran
23. 5. 2016

Shakespeare Now!

Series edited by Ewan Fernie and Simon Palfrey

Web editors: Theodora Papadopoulou and William McKenzie

Visit the *Shakespeare Now!* Blog at http://shakespearenowseries.blogspot.com/ for further news and updates on the series.

Shakespeare's Universality

Here's Fine Revolution

KIERNAN RYAN

Bloomsbury Arden Shakespeare
An imprint of Bloomsbury Publishing Plc

B L O O M S B U R Y

LONDON • NEW DELHI • NEW YORK • SYDNEY

Bloomsbury Arden Shakespeare

An imprint of Bloomsbury Publishing Plc

Imprint previously known as Arden Shakespeare

50 Bedford Square	1385 Broadway
London	New York
WC1B 3DP	NY 10018
UK	USA

www.bloomsbury.com

BLOOMSBURY, THE ARDEN SHAKESPEARE and the Diana logo are trademarks of Bloomsbury Publishing Plc

First published 2015

© Kiernan Ryan, 2015

Kiernan Ryan has asserted his right under the Copyright, Designs and Patents Act, 1988, to be identified as author of this work.

British Library Cataloguing-in-Publication Data
A catalogue record for this book is available from the British Library.

ISBN: PB:978-1-4081-8349-6
ePDF:978-1-4725-0326-8
ePub:978-1-4725-0325-1

Library of Congress Cataloging-in-Publication Data
A catalog record for this book is available from the Library of Congress.

Series: Shakespeare Now!

Typeset by Fakenham Prepress Solutions, Fakenham, Norfolk NR21 8NN
Printed and bound in Great Britain

For Liz

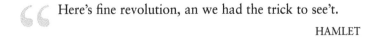

If I say, therefore, that Shakespeare is the greatest of Intellects, I have said all concerning him. But there is more in Shakespeare's intellect than we have yet seen. It is what I call an unconscious intellect; there is more virtue in it than he himself is aware of. ... Whoever looks intelligently at this Shakespeare may recognize that he too was a Prophet, in his way; of an insight analogous to the Prophetic, though he took it up in another strain ... We call Dante the melodious Priest of Middle-Age Catholicism. May we not call Shakespeare the still more melodious Priest of a true Catholicism, the 'Universal Church' of the Future and of all times?

THOMAS CARLYLE, *'The Hero as Poet'*

Here's fine revolution, an we had the trick to see't.

HAMLET

CONTENTS

GENERAL EDITORS' PREFACE

We begin with the passions of the critic as they are forged and explored in Shakespeare. These books speak directly from that fundamental experience of losing and remaking yourself in art. This does not imply, necessarily, a lonely existentialism; the story of a self is always bound up in other stories, shared tales of nations or faiths or of families large and small. But such stories are also always singular, irreducible to the generalities by which they are typically explained. Here, then, is where literary experience stops pretending to provide institutionalized objectivity, and starts to tell its own story.

Shakespeare Now! is a rallying cry, above all for aesthetic immediacy. It favours a model of aesthetic knowledge as *encounter,* where the encounter brings its own, often surprising contextualizing imperatives. Implicit in this is the premise that art is as much a subject as an object, less like aggregated facts and more like a fascinating person or persons. And encountering the plays as such is unavoidably personal.

Much recent scholarship has been devoted to Shakespeare *then* – to producing more information about the presumed moment of their inception. But this moment of inception is in truth happening over and over, again and again, anywhere that Shakespeare is being experienced anew or freshly. For the fact is that he remains, by a country mile, the most important *contemporary* writer – the most performed and read, the most written about, but also the most remembered. But it is not a question merely of Shakespeare in the present, as though his vitality is best measured by his passing relevance to great events. It is about his works' abiding *presence*.

In some ways criticism needs to get younger – to recover the freshness of aesthetic experience, and so in part better to remember why any of us should care. We need a new directness, written responses to the plays which attest to the life we find in them and the life they find in us.

Ewan Fernie and Simon Palfrey

PREFACE

This book sets out to reclaim the concept of Shakespeare's universality from the reactionary misconstructions that have been placed on it by conservative and radical critics alike. The source of Shakespeare's enduring appeal, not just in his native land but in countries all over the world, has been widely regarded for centuries as the result of his genius for dramatizing the timeless truths of the universal human condition. The grip of this explanation on the minds of most students, teachers and lovers of Shakespeare across the globe remains, for want of a more compelling reason, tenacious to this day, notwithstanding repeated attempts in recent decades to reject the idea of Shakespeare's universality as an intellectually indefensible and politically pernicious myth.

For the past 30 years or so the very idea has been viewed as taboo in academic quarters, where any suggestion that one might wish to take it seriously is enough to invite derision. The overriding imperative for Shakespeare studies during this period has been to demonstrate that his drama was not 'for all time', as Ben Jonson famously claimed, but 'of an age', and that only by restoring it to that age, and embedding it as deeply as possibly in its historical milieu, can it be properly understood. Scholars and critics bent on hastening 'The Demise of the Transcendent Bard' (as one of them dubbed it) by historicizing his works have also been motivated, more often than not, by a desire to demolish a conception of Shakespeare that has for too long been ideologically complicit, they would argue, in perpetuating social, sexual and racial injustice.

Nor has this desire remained confined to the academy that has done so much to foster it. The World Shakespeare Festival staged at the Globe in 2012, the year of the London Olympics, provoked an angry article by Emer O'Toole in the *Guardian* of 21 May headed 'Shakespeare, universal? No, it's cultural imperialism'. 'Shakespeare is full of classism, sexism, racism and defunct social mores', fumed O'Toole. '*The Taming of the Shrew* (aka The Shaming of the Vagina-Bearer) is about as universally relevant as the chastity belt', while '*The Merchant of Venice* (or The Evil Jew) is about as universal as the Nuremberg laws.' 'So where', O'Toole asked, 'has the idea that Shakespeare is "universal" come from? Why do people the world over study and perform Shakespeare? Colonialism. That's where, and that's why. Shakespeare was a powerful tool of empire, transported to foreign climes along with the doctrine of European cultural superiority.'

The strident tone of O'Toole's tirade may not be to everyone's taste, but her assault on the notion that his plays still matter because there's something inherently universal about the stories they tell is as justified as her mockery of productions that try to wriggle round the repugnant opinions characters voice in them, and her charge that the alleged universality of the tales he dramatized played a key role in making Shakespeare's drama 'a powerful tool of empire'. The contention that *The Taming of the Shrew*, *The Merchant of Venice*, or any other play by Shakespeare has the capacity to appeal to people in all times and places, whatever their nationality, race, gender, language, creed or sexual orientation, because it reflects a universal experience that everyone can identify with or relate to, doesn't stand up to scrutiny for a moment. For millions of people in all parts of the world, Shakespeare holds no appeal whatsoever and for a host of obvious reasons, but it's certainly not because they haven't yet discovered that his drama distils the essence of humanity, and thus holds a mirror up to the lives of everyone everywhere.

Shakespeare's drama patently does no such thing, not least because the subject matter it deals with, the forms it takes and the language it uses mark it out immediately as the product of the age in which it was written. To the extent that it's succeeded in hammering that fact home, the concerted academic endeavour in recent decades to historicize Shakespeare, and thus spike the toxic myth of the 'Transcendent Bard', is to be applauded. The trouble with those engaged in this enterprise, however, and the trouble with those who share Emer O'Toole's views, is that in their keenness to spike that myth they haven't stopped to consider whether the extraordinary endurance and scale of Shakespeare's international appeal are due to his drama's being 'universal' and thus 'timeless' in a sense quite different from the usual meaning of those terms when applied to it – a sense perfectly compatible with its anchorage in the age of Shakespeare. As a consequence, they have rendered themselves incapable of credibly explaining why Shakespeare's appeal has endured for so long, and his global cultural impact has continued to expand exponentially, while the works of his fellow dramatists remain for the most part marooned in the distant past, are rarely if ever performed, and are of abiding interest only to scholars. More importantly, however, they have robbed Shakespeare's plays of the very qualities that empower them to dramatize his time from a vantage point that's still far ahead of our time rather than immured in the antiquated attitudes, however iniquitous or innocuous, of the early modern world.

Previous attempts to defend the idea of Shakespeare's timeless universality on grounds other than the standard, transparently spurious one have signally failed to gain traction. In an article entitled 'Shakespeare's globe', which appeared in the *Telegraph* of 23 April 2012, a month before Emer O'Toole's *Guardian* piece and prompted by the prospect of the same World Shakespeare Festival that aroused O'Toole's wrath, Jonathan Bate posed the question: 'What is the source of the universal appeal of this balding middle-class gentleman, born in a little Warwickshire town in the reign of the first Queen Elizabeth?' His answer begins conventionally enough by proposing that 'the key to his universality' lies in his drama's accommodation of both 'permanent truths and historical contingencies': Shakespeare 'worked with archetypal characters, core plots and perennial conflicts, but at the same time 'he also addressed the conflicts of his own historical moment'. The plays bring alive, in other words, the experiences, ideas and issues peculiar to their era, but beneath the historical contingencies can be discerned the permanent truths they embody, which make the plays universally intelligible. Having dispatched this version of the same old explanation, however, Bate changes tack and advances an altogether different reason for Shakespeare's refusal to become obsolete:

> Because Shakespeare was supremely attuned to his own historical moment, but never wholly constrained within it, his works lived on after his death through something similar to the Darwinian principle of adaptation. The key to Darwin's theory of evolution is the survival of the fittest. Species survive according to their capacity to adapt, to evolve according to environmental circumstances. As with natural selection, the quality that makes a really successful, enduring cultural artefact is its capacity to change in response to new circumstances. Shakespeare's plays, because they are so various and so open to interpretation, so lacking in dogma, have achieved this trick more fully than any other work of the human imagination.

I share Bate's belief that Shakespeare's works have lived on so long after his death 'Because Shakespeare was supremely attuned to his own historical moment, but never wholly constrained within it'. I part company with him, however, when he contends that Shakespeare was never wholly constrained within his historical moment because his plays are 'so open to interpretation' that succeeding generations have been able to read into them whatever the circumstances of the day demand.

That succeeding generations have interpreted Shakespeare's plays in different ways for diverse reasons is undeniable, but that fact doesn't warrant the inference Bate draws from it. The notion that the enduring, world-wide appeal of Shakespeare's drama is down to its being so blandly non-committal and infinitely accommodating that it will allow any expedient reading to be imposed on it is surely no more credible than ascribing it to the plays' portrayal of the permanent truths of the human condition tricked out as historical contingencies. Indeed, in my view it's precisely the profound commitment of Shakespeare's drama to the emancipation of humanity that enables it to dramatize the historical reality of his age from an imaginative standpoint in the transfigured future human beings are still struggling to create. What is universal about Shakespeare's drama is not the plights and fates of his characters, but the perspective from which they are depicted, and from which we are invited to view them. To grasp the true source and significance of Shakespeare's universality, moreover, is to grasp the real reason why the plays have outlived the world they body forth, and thus the respect in which they may justifiably be described as timeless. It's also to understand the power that Shakespeare's dramatic art possesses to keep the dream of revolutionary transformation alive today.

That is the gist of what I contend in this book, which is divided into four chapters. The first chapter outlines the argument, and the rest of the book develops it in detail through close readings and discussions of a wide range of plays and poems. Chapter 2 focuses in depth on the timeless aspect of Shakespeare's drama, which is indivisible from the question of its universality, to which the third and longest chapter is devoted. And the last chapter recapitulates the key points of the book's argument through a reading of *Timon of Athens*, in which bizarre, ostensibly anomalous play, I suggest, the quintessential qualities of Shakespearean drama are enshrined.

I'm fortunate to have had the opportunity to test and tighten up the basic argument of this book in lectures at various venues. Earlier versions of the opening chapter were delivered, under diverse titles, at the international symposium on 'Shakespeare's Adaptability' at the University of Thessaloniki;

at the international symposium on 'World Shakespeare: Teaching, Translation, Performance' at the University of Athens; at the Bibliotheca Alexandrina, Alexandria, Egypt; at the colloquium on 'Literary and Economic Signifiers' at the University of Geneva; at the conference on 'La Differenza di Shakespeare' at the University of Bergamo; at the Hull Literary and Philosophical Society, Kingston upon Hull; and as the inaugural Annual Public Shakespeare Lecture, jointly sponsored by the Abbey Theatre and University College Dublin, at the Global Irish Institute, UCD. I owe special thanks to Tina Krontiris, Aspasia Velissariou, Ismail Serageldin, Rick Waswo, Alessandra Marzola, Susann Chambers and Jane Grogan for their invitations to speak and their warm hospitality.

Some of the ideas in Chapters 2 and 4 have benefited from being previously aired in a lecture delivered at the International Shakespeare Association conference on 'Working with Shakespeare' at the Shakespeare Institute, Stratford upon Avon and in the F. W. Bateson Memorial Lecture at Corpus Christi College, Oxford. I am especially grateful to the President of Corpus, Richard Carwardine, for the invitation to deliver the Bateson Lecture and for the warmth of the welcome my wife Liz and I received on this occasion. Chapter 3 incorporates some points and revised versions of passages in the Annual Public Shakespeare Lecture I delivered at the University of Hull at the kind invitation of Janet Clare, and in the keynote lecture I gave at the annual conference of the Romanian Society for English & American Studies at the equally kind invitation of the Director of the Romanian Cultural Institute, Dorian Branea. The reading of *Timon of Athens* in Chapter 4 profited immensely from the feedback I received on a seminar paper given at the Shakespeare Institute in Stratford.

Earlier versions of parts of the argument of Chapter 1 were published as 'Pagosmios Saixpir: e politiki tis ikiopoiesis', in *E Prosarmostikotita tou Saixpir* [*Shakespeare's Adaptability*], ed. Tina Krontiris (Athens: Ergo, 2004) and as 'Shakespeare's

Universality: The Politics of Appropriation', in *The Difference of Shakespeare*, ed. Alessandra Marzola (Bergamo: Bergamo University Press, 2008). Chapters 2 and 4 incorporate some rejigged extracts from my essay '"Here's fine revolution": Shakespeare's Philosophy of the Future', *Essays in Criticism*, 63:2 (April 2013), and a few revamped paragraphs from my essay 'Shakespeare's Inhumanity' in *Shakespeare Survey 66* (2013) have been spliced into Chapter 3. I've also taken the liberty of adapting and recycling in Chapter 3 some material from the chapters on *A Midsummer Night's Dream*, *As You Like It* and *Twelfth Night* in my book *Shakespeare's Comedies* (Basingstoke: Palgrave Macmillan, 2009). Although that book is not explicitly concerned with Shakespeare's universality, further corroboration of the argument of this book can be found in the detailed readings of the comedies it provides.

To free this brief polemic of footnotes I've kept primary and secondary references to the bare minimum and confined those not included in the chapters themselves to a separate section ('Works Cited') at the back of the book.

Finally, I wish to thank the editors of *Shakespeare Now!*, Ewan Fernie and Simon Palfrey, for inviting me to contribute this book to the series, and Margaret Bartley for her invaluable encouragement and legendary forbearance during its writing.

CHAPTER ONE

Reclaiming Shakespeare's Universality

I

The twin paradoxes that still bedevil the interpretation of Shakespeare's plays and the justification of his supremacy were first framed in 1623 by Ben Jonson in the poem he supplied for the First Folio: 'To the memory of my beloved, The AUTHOR MR. WILLIAM SHAKESPEARE: AND what he hath left us.' That phrase emphatically bolted onto the poem's title by Jonson, 'AND what he hath left us', defines Shakespeare's drama, at the start of its voyage through time, as a legacy whose significance and value it's our task, as the dramatist's heirs, to determine. As far as Jonson's concerned, Shakespeare's pre-eminence as a playwright is self-evident, and the reasons for his apotheosis beyond dispute. Jonson praises Shakespeare as the epitome of his birthplace and nation, as the 'Sweet swan of Avon' and 'the wonder of our stage'. Yet he's also a playwright 'To whom all scenes of Europe homage owe', who belongs not only in the front rank of his English contemporaries, but also in the international pantheon of the mighty Greek dramatists and their continental heirs, and thus to the world. Jonson is equally keen to hail Shakespeare as the 'Soul of the age', the essence of the era in which he wrote; yet he also acclaims him as an immortal 'monument without a tomb', the 'star of poets', who is 'not of an age, but for all time!'

Local yet global, rooted in the past yet perpetually present: the double paradox through which Jonson defined Shakespeare's achievement still sets the agenda for debate 400 years on. The problem is that Jonson's complex grasp of the matter has been discarded by most subsequent critics, who have polarized into two hostile camps, each of which labours under a lopsided view of the response Shakespeare's drama demands. On the one hand, we have those who are wedded to the notion of a transcendent Bard, whose plays have withstood the trials of time and triumphed in translation all over the world, because they express with matchless eloquence and dramatic power the unchanging truths of the universal human condition. On the other, we find those who insist that Shakespeare is categorically not for all time, but inextricably of his age, and that to uproot his writings from the time and place from which they sprang, and treat their author as our ageless contemporary, is to rob them of their revelations about a vanished world that is radically different from our own.

For the last four centuries, the transcendent Bard has undoubtedly prevailed over the time-bound Bard. From Samuel Johnson to Coleridge to Harold Bloom, Shakespeare's ability to shake off the shackles of history by virtue of his drama's universality has found powerful advocates, whose views are shared by the vast majority of students, teachers and lovers of Shakespeare around the world to this day. 'Nothing can please many, and please long,' wrote Dr Johnson, 'but just representations of general nature.' Shakespeare's characters, he went on,

> are not modified by the customs of particular places, unpractised by the rest of the world ... or by the accidents of transient fashions or temporary opinions: they are the genuine progeny of common humanity, such as the world will always supply and observation will always find ...

> In the writings of other poets a character is too often an individual; in those of Shakespeare it is commonly a species.

For Coleridge, 'our myriad-minded Shakespeare' is 'the great, ever living, dead man', because 'he is of no age – nor ... of any religion, or party, or profession. The body and substance of his works came out of the unfathomable depths of his own oceanic mind.' Coleridge attributes Shakespeare's perennial, ubiquitous appeal to the creative capaciousness of his mind (what G. K. Chesterton would later call his 'mental hospitality'), whereas Dr Johnson ascribes it to Shakespeare's faithful recreation of the common human nature he observed around him. But for both men the universal scope of his dramatic vision is a matter of fact, not a matter for debate. And over 200 years later, at the close of the twentieth century, Harold Bloom can be found donning the mantle of Dr Johnson in his bestseller *Shakespeare: The Invention of the Human*, whose first chapter is defiantly entitled 'Shakespeare's Universalism'.

Bloom's defiance is directed at the historicist criticism that has ruled the academic roost in Shakespeare studies, and in literary studies in general, for the past 30 years, and that continues to rule it despite valiant efforts to topple it from its perch. Historicist critics of Shakespeare come in a variety of hues, but they are united in their hostility to the idea of Shakespeare's timeless universality, and their insistence on anchoring the plays in the age and culture in which they were written in order to understand them properly. In blithe contempt of that insistence, Bloom is equally adamant that Shakespeare has become 'the first universal author, replacing the Bible in the secularised consciousness. Attempts to historicize his ascendancy continue to founder on the uniqueness of his eminence, for the cultural factors critics find relevant to Shakespeare are precisely as relevant to Thomas Dekker and to George Chapman.' Bloom's objection to historicist accounts of Shakespeare – on this ground at least – is irrefutable, since even the most comprehensive, densely detailed recreation of the culture that cradled Shakespeare and his fellow dramatists can't begin to explain why Shakespeare's plays have bewitched the world, while theirs are seldom or never performed and of interest only to academics.

The school of criticism Bloom excoriates has remained undeterred, however, by what most of its members dismissed as a reactionary, last-ditch defence of 'Universal Shakespeare'. Nor is it difficult to see why, if one concedes the force of their case in its most politically progressive form. For there's no denying that the idea of Shakespeare's timeless universality has been used overwhelmingly in the past for reactionary ends: to make class society, patriarchy, racial divisions and colonial domination vanish behind the smokescreen of the eternal human predicament his drama allegedly reflects. Whereas to read Shakespeare historically, so scholars and critics of this camp contend – to return his plays to the milieu that moulded them, and embed them in the class-divided, patriarchal, white Western culture of their time – is not only to confront their complicity with that culture and shatter the myth of their timeless universality, but also to restore Shakespeare's distance and difference from us, and thus both the historical fact, and the future possibility, of change.

So persuasive has this argument proved that – in academic circles at least, if nowhere else – all talk of Shakespeare's universality and transcendence of history has become strictly taboo. As Leah Marcus wrote back in the 1980s in *Puzzling Shakespeare*, her influential manifesto for 'localizing' his drama: 'Shakespeare's "universal" temper and "oceanic mind" have been enshrined for so long that these concepts, once so thrilling for readers and critics, now function less to preserve the vitality of the figure we call Shakespeare than to condemn it to slow asphyxiation.' Along with her fellow historicists in the US and their counterparts in Britain, Marcus proclaimed 'The Demise of the Transcendent Bard' and the birth of a Bard steeped in history and thus vulnerable to political critique. And at the close of the twentieth century another distinguished American academic, David Scott Kastan, in his manifesto for Shakespeare studies in the twenty-first century, called for Shakespeare scholars to entrench his plays even more deeply in the past: 'to restore Shakespeare's artistry to the earliest conditions of its realization and intelligibility: to the collaborations of the book trade in which [the plays] were published, to the unstable political world of late Tudor and early Stuart England in which the plays were engaged by their various publics'. It requires no more than a glance at the catalogues of most university presses, and at the research projects that secure doctoral and postdoctoral funding, to confirm that this objective, in one form or another, still sets the main agenda for Shakespeare studies in the universities of the English-speaking world. Most recent and current academic work on Shakespeare's drama is concerned with what it once meant to people long since dead in a world that no longer exists, or with what it has been made to mean in subsequent eras by diverse cultures; which has left those academics who bridle at this past-bound, retrospective approach to the plays little choice but to reinterpret them from the perspective of the present instead, regardless of their supposed original import and the scorn of historicist scholarship.

It would be churlish to deny that the conquest of modern Shakespeare studies by historicist criticism has much to commend it. Its exponents have enriched our understanding of Shakespeare and his world by splicing the plays back into neglected cultural contexts and exposing their collusion in, as well as their resistance to, social, sexual and racial injustice in their time. In the process they have dealt a severe, though far from fatal, blow to the complacent assumption that Shakespeare's drama enshrines the abiding truths of the human condition. But in dealing that blow they have sentenced Shakespeare's drama to languish in the prison-house of the past, immured in their late modern conception of the early modern era. The most obvious problem with this approach to Shakespeare is its powerlessness to account for his expanding appeal over the last four centuries to the most disparate cultures across the globe – an appeal that owes nothing to the knowledge of the period and society in which he wrote that historicist scholars consider *de rigueur* for understanding his plays. Of course, the cynical reason offered in some academic circles for Shakespeare's enduring supremacy and global reach is his drama's efficacy as a covert instrument of ideological indoctrination and cultural imperialism, rather than its possession of intrinsic virtues that override the nefarious ends it has been made to serve. That argument patently won't wash, however: not just because it posits in the peoples of the world a capacity for sustained self-delusion on an implausible scale, but because it can't credibly explain why such a wealth of creative and critical energy has been invested by so many different cultures for so long in the works of Shakespeare rather than in the works of any other author of any era.

The question of what sets Shakespeare apart, and why he remains the keystone of the canon of world literature, and a constant source of inspiration for theatre directors, film makers, playwrights, poets, novelists, composers, choreographers and painters around the globe, is still in quest of an answer. If it's not because Shakespeare dramatizes the perennial plight of all human beings everywhere, and if embedding his plays in the epoch that engendered them can't explain their refusal to stay put in their time and their country of origin, then we need to search elsewhere.

II

I think we need to take a fresh look at the critically discredited concepts of Shakespeare's universality and timelessness, and see if we can reclaim them from the misconceptions to which they continue to be subjected. For if we could show that the quality of timeless universality *in a progressive sense* is inherent in the plays – genetically stored in their language and form from the start – then we would have a much more compelling rationale for radical reinterpretations of them on stage and screen and in secondary and higher education. After all, the idea that there's something universal and timeless about Shakespeare's drama has proved formidably resilient over the last 400 years, and recent academic attempts to dismiss it as a pernicious, moth-eaten myth have failed to persuade the vast majority of the world's Shakespeare-lovers, for whom the idea continues to have the ring of self-evident truth. The fact that it does should give those who deride the idea pause before they put it down to gullibility, ignorance or ideological brainwashing. I believe that it still rings true to most students, theatregoers and performers because it describes an actual effect the plays have on them, an effect produced by the way the plays are constructed and worded. That Shakespeare's plays possess, as has been widely agreed for centuries, a timeless, universal quality is not the problem. The problem is the *conservative construction* that has been placed on this quality, and the reactionary purposes for which it has been employed, by conservative critics, and by conservative cultural and educational institutions, since the eighteenth century.

Insofar as the wrath of the militant anti-universalists has been directed at this reactionary *misconception* of Shakespeare's universality and dedicated to demolishing it, they are plainly to be commended. For it has unquestionably been a crucial factor in what Denis Kennedy has decried as 'the enforced study of Shakespeare in Britain and America', which 'has long been used ... to support traditionalist notions of class distinctions, the merit of high art, the social worth of advanced education, and the value of the arcane'. And it undoubtedly underpinned the exportation of the Bard to the farthest reaches of the British Empire, and particularly the Indian subcontinent, in order to illustrate the linguistic and cultural superiority of the invader. Yet it requires merely a moment's reflection on the facts of the matter to dispose of the delusion that Shakespeare's drama is universal in the sense that it appeals equally to every nation on Earth. What

Kennedy concluded in his Afterword to *Foreign Shakespeare* 20 years ago remains just as true today: 'Any approach to Shakespeare that inquires about his prevalence in world culture is obliged to notice that he is not valued everywhere. Claims of Shakespeare's universality cannot be substantiated, at least on a literal level, since there are numerous areas in which he is not read, performed, or studied with enthusiasm: by the enormous populations of the Islamic countries, for instance (where no dramatist is highly valued, though poets certainly are), in much of South-east Asia, in most of Africa.'

The claim that the appeal of Shakespeare's drama is literally universal is patently too absurd to merit further consideration. But the more seductive claim that Shakespeare's drama is universal, and thus timeless, because it reflects the essential human condition of everyone who *does* read, perform or study it, whatever their nationality, race, age, class, gender or sexual orientation, is equally unconvincing because no less obviously untrue, and its conscription to mask inequality and injustice of every kind has rightly been exposed and deplored. When Jane Smiley rewrote *King Lear*, in her Pulitzer-Prize-winning novel *A Thousand Acres*, to update and retell the story from the demonized daughters' point of view, she made it plain that her prime target was 'Mr Shakespeare's alleged universality', a myth contrived to disguise the patriarchal point of view as the common plight of humanity. If the criterion of universality is giving *equal representation* to the experience and viewpoint of every sector of society, so that all readers or spectators can find their counterparts in characters with whom they can identify, and in whose fate they can see their own mirrored, then it's a criterion that Shakespeare's drama spectacularly fails to meet. On these grounds, iconoclastic creative assaults on Shakespeare like Smiley's, and the academic drive to tether him to his time, are justified and long overdue. Nor is it hard to understand how readily the desire to demystify can mutate into the sarcastic contempt vented in Franco Moretti's classic critique of Shakespearean tragedy in *Signs Taken for Wonders*: 'It should be clear that this Shakespearean "poetry" has nothing "liberating", "constructive" or "universal" about it, but is just Shakespeare's response to the crisis of class society in his time and the tragic disenchantment it produced.'

The trouble is that the authors of these justified dismissals of Shakespeare's universality as a historically explicable ideological illusion, whose function has been to conceal social, sexual and racial divisions, never pause to wonder whether the plays might have possessed this quality all along in a quite different sense, which the conservative construction imposed upon it has obscured. There's a vital distinction to be drawn between the reactionary concept of universalism, to which radical modern critics rightly object, and the *revolutionary universalism* that first found full philosophical and political expression in the Enlightenment, but which, I would argue, had already found *imaginative* expression in the plays of Shakespeare, as that notoriously bardolatrous political philosopher Karl Marx wasn't slow to realize. This revolutionary universalism is dramatically and poetically articulated in Shakespeare's plays, which reveal the *potential* of all human beings to live according to principles of freedom, equality and justice. It is *revolutionary* because the fulfilment of that potential implicitly demands the complete transformation of the terms on which people lived in Shakespeare's day and tragically, in so many ways, still live today.

It's my contention that this profound commitment to the *universal human potential* to live otherwise is the secret of the plays' proven ability to transcend their time. This is what drives their radical dissatisfaction with Shakespeare's world, divorcing their vision from the assumptions and attitudes that held sway in early modern England, and opening them up to the future and the prospect of the world transfigured. That prospect – the tidal pull of futurity that inflects their language and form at every turn – is what propels Shakespeare's plays beyond the horizon of his age to speak with more authority and power than ever to ours. The timelessness of the plays springs from their refusal to make complete sense in the terms of their time, which they view from the vantage point of a future we ourselves can only imagine. Let me be absolutely clear: I am not suggesting that Shakespeare's quintessentially Elizabethan and Jacobean plays miraculously dissolve, as we watch or read them, revealing the primordial bedrock of human nature that persists forever beneath the surface of social change. On the contrary: Shakespeare dramatizes the intractable reality of his world in such vividly realized, sensuous detail, in such unprecedented depth, and with such articulate energy, that the plays transport our imaginations back to the age in which they were written, an age whose indelible imprint can be traced in every line. But he dramatizes that early modern reality in such a way as to reveal the potential it harbours for transformation, the potential of human beings, then and now, to base their lives together on values that possess universal validity, because they are founded on the simple, irrefutable fact that we belong to the same species.

Ben Jonson's paradoxical praise of Shakespeare as *both* the 'Soul of the age' *and yet* 'not of an age, but for all time', as *both* the epitome of his birthplace and nation *and* global in his impact and significance, makes complete sense when understood in these terms. Shakespeare captures the 'Soul of the age' in his plays in a way that transcends his age, because he writes about his age from an imaginative perspective that's ahead of his time, not confined to it. Insofar as that universal perspective is still ahead of our time, moreover, Shakespeare's dramatic dispatches from that distant past still have the power to activate visions of alternative futures today. To put it another way, Ben Jonson's Augustan namesake couldn't have been more wrong when he wrote that Shakespeare's characters 'are not modified by the customs of particular places, unpractised by the rest of the world ... or by the accidents of transient fashions or temporary opinions: they are the genuine progeny of common humanity, such as the world will always supply and observation will always find'. What the good Doctor should have written is: 'Shakespeare's characters are so vivid and unforgettable precisely because they *are* modified by the customs of particular places and by the accidents of transient fashions and temporary opinions; but they are dramatized *from the perspective of* 'common humanity' – from the anticipated future perspective of a genuinely universal human community no longer crippled by division and domination.

III

Emerson caught this *anachronistic* aspect of Shakespeare's dramatic art – its alienation from the age in which it was written *and* from the subsequent ages in which it has so far been staged and studied – when he observed that Shakespeare is 'as unlike his cotemporaries as he is unlike us'. In other words, the tragedies, comedies and histories are out of sync with both Shakespeare's epoch and ours, and so can't be *completely* explained in terms either of the past that produced them or the present in which we encounter them, which is why neither a historicist nor a presentist critical approach will suffice to do them justice. Emerson owed his trenchant insight directly to Coleridge, who was the first to grasp this feature of the plays, and thus lay the foundations for transforming our understanding of their past significance and their present meaning. Coleridge, like Dr Johnson, has been a mine of quotations for critics keen to buttress the bland conservative version of Shakespeare's universality. But on closer inspection he turns out to have a much more complex and illuminating explanation of why the glove-maker's lad from Stratford has lasted so long.

Shakespeare, Coleridge realized, 'writes not for past ages but for that in which he lives and that which is to follow. It is natural that he should conform to the circumstances of his day, but a true genius will stand independent of these circumstances.' 'It is a poor compliment to a poet', Coleridge remarks, with Shakespeare specifically in mind, 'to tell him that he has only the qualifications of an historian' – a remark which critics and scholars of a historicist bent might do well to ponder. What allows Shakespeare's plays to stand independent of the historical circumstances to which they otherwise conform is not their portrayal of an essential order of things that never changes, or essential human types 'such as the world will always supply and observation will always find', but the dream of 'that which is to follow'. When we engage with imaginative writing, Coleridge explains, 'we wish to have a shadow, a sort of prophetic existence present to us, which tells us what we are not, but yet, blending in us much that we are, promises great things of what we may be'. The plays of Shakespeare cast the shadow of that 'prophetic existence', and it's in this sense that Shakespeare, in Coleridge's superb phrase, 'shakes off the iron bondage of space and time'; while he 'registers what is past, he projects the future in a wonderful degree'.

The other great Romantic critic of Shakespeare, Hazlitt, latched on to this prophetic propensity of the plays too. 'Chaucer most frequently describes things as they are', he wrote, 'Spenser, as we wish them to be; Shakespeare, as they would be'. Like Coleridge, Hazlitt recognized that the meaning and value of the plays can't be restricted to what they meant, and why they mattered, in their original historical milieu. 'This play has a prophetic truth,' he declared of *Hamlet*, 'which is above that of history.' But unlike Coleridge, Hazlitt also discerned the profoundly democratic thrust of Shakespeare's dramatic imagination; and thus, even though he couldn't fully grasp the link between that democratic imagination and the future the plays presaged, Hazlitt paved the way for the realization that their refusal to stay entrenched in their time is inextricable from their 'myriad-minded', universalizing depiction of their time:

> The striking peculiarity of Shakespeare's mind was its generic quality, its power of communication with all other minds – so that it contained a universe of thought and feeling within itself, and had no one peculiar bias,

or exclusive excellence more than another. ... He was nothing in himself; but he was all that others were, or that they could become. He not only had in himself the germs of every faculty and feeling, but he could follow them by anticipation, intuitively, into all their conceivable ramifications, through every change of fortune or conflict of passion, or turn of thought. He had 'a mind reflecting ages past', and present: – all the people that ever lived are there. There was no respect of persons with him. His genius shone equally on the evil and on the good, on the wise and the foolish, the monarch and the beggar: 'All corners of the earth, kings, queens, and states, maids, matrons, nay, the secrets of the grave', are hardly hid from his searching glance.

Once the bardolatrous hyperbole has been filtered out of these remarks, two crucial intuitions remain that point to the revolutionary nature of Shakespeare's universality.

The first is latent in that phrase about his mind's 'generic quality, its power of communication with all other minds'. This strikes me as a very productive idea, because it redefines Shakespeare's universality as a *capacity for communication*, for creating and addressing a community of minds united in a common cause. The implication is that Shakespeare's universality is not a property of his subject matter, but *an effect of the perspective from which he presents it and invites us to perceive it*. In other words, it's not that the story of Richard II, Hamlet or Prospero secretes the universal story of mankind; it's that their stories are told from a 'generic' point of view that cuts across the distinctions and divisions forged by history, nationality, race, religion, language, class, gender and sexuality. So when we're watching *Twelfth Night*, *Antony and Cleopatra*, or *The Winter's Tale*, we're not seeing the essential condition of humanity in all times and places, which an eighteenth-century Buddhist monk in Tibet, a Turkish-born cleaning lady from Cologne, or a gay African-American stockbroker would all recognize as their own. What we're seeing is an irreducibly singular drama, about these idiosyncratic individuals, who speak and act in distinctive ways, and in forms of language, that stamp the play as a unique product of the place and time in which Shakespeare penned it. But that drama is shaped and phrased in such a way as to activate our awareness of the *potential* we share with the protagonists, and with all human beings then and now, to live more fulfilling lives than those we find ourselves compelled to live by the place and time we happen to inhabit.

Hazlitt's second key intuition is summarized in the sentence: 'His genius shone equally on the evil and on the good, on the wise and the foolish, the monarch and the beggar.' Shakespeare's 'power of communication with all other minds', the power to ignite an awareness of the *potential* universally possessed by humankind, is indivisible from the democratic attitude of his drama. The sense of boundless human potentiality that pulses through the plays is reflected in Hazlitt's claim that Shakespeare 'was all that others were, *or that they could become*', because he possessed 'the *germs* of every faculty and feeling', which he could follow '*by anticipation*, intuitively, into all their conceivable ramifications'. At the same time, Shakespeare's capacity to anticipate imaginatively through his characters all that others 'could become' hinges for Hazlitt on his gift for depicting 'all that others were'. The fact that Shakespeare 'had "a mind reflecting ages past", and present' is yoked to his ability to enshrine in his plays prophetic truths that are above the truths of history. This tension between the actual and the potential, between reflecting what has been and foreshadowing what could be, is bound up in turn, Hazlitt senses, with the levelling impulse that led Shakespeare to shine his genius equally on monarchs and beggars, because 'There was no respect of persons with him.' To put the point hatched by Hazlitt another way: the characters of Shakespeare's comedies, histories and tragedies inhabit imaginary worlds, which are just as class-divided, misogynistic, racist and heterosexually biased as the Renaissance reality Shakespeare transmutes into poetic drama. How could they not be? But those worlds are dramatized from a perspective rooted in the recognition of the fundamental equality of all human beings. The plays invite us to view the way things were in Shakespeare's time from *an egalitarian standpoint* that is still in advance of our time.

This universal human standpoint is forged most obviously, but not solely, by Shakespeare's keenness to exploit the polyphonic possibilities of his dramatic medium more fully than any of his fellow playwrights. The hallmark of Shakespeare's levelling imagination for Hazlitt is his conscription of that multivocal medium to give a voice to the monarch King Lear *and* the beggar Poor Tom; to Prince Hamlet *and* the grave-digger; to Macbeth *and* the drunken porter; to Duke Theseus *and* Bottom the weaver; to anti-Semitic Christians *and* the Jew Shylock; to Henry V *and* a disaffected foot-soldier on the eve of battle; to the exiled Duke Prospero *and* his slave Caliban, whose island he stole. Women and men, the ruled and the rulers, servants and masters, the foreign and the native, gods, witches and fairies, the vicious and the virtuous: the right of utterance is distributed across the whole spectrum of roles and relationships, without privileging any point of view or set of values over the others. As A. L. French concluded half a century ago in his essay '*Hamlet* and the Moralists': 'in any given piece the points of view add up to a total vision of human behaviour which is not identical with the vision that any one character has'.

The covert effect of Shakespeare's multivocal mode of composition is to create, and invite us to adopt, a common human perspective, which dissolves the assumptions that underpin the hierarchical society his drama depicts. 'The art of Shakespeare', John Bayley observes in *Shakespeare and Tragedy*, 'draws attention to how free we are from its own material and manipulation' compared to his characters: 'The play that frees our spirits has cabined and confined theirs, enclosed them within the walls of predicament.' Although the last thing on Bayley's mind is the political import of this aspect of Shakespeare's art, his observation points to the crucial distinction to be drawn between the experience of the characters locked inside the play and the spectator's experience of emotional and mental deliverance from their dramatized predicament. Although the minds, speech and deeds of Shakespeare's *dramatis personae* are fated to remain in thrall to the dehumanizing divisions that still prevail in the real world outside the theatre, the universal perspective from which the play portrays their fate opens up the *prospect* of equality and community for the *audience*. Franco Moretti couldn't have been more wrong, in short, when he declared that 'this Shakespearean "poetry" has nothing "liberating", "constructive" or "universal" about it'. Full human equality and genuine community, despite the huge strides taken towards achieving them in some parts of the world since Shakespeare's day, remain a shamefully distant prospect in our time. The fact that they do makes the active enlistment of his drama's revolutionary universality – the quality that empowers it to speak more urgently to us than any modern drama can – more imperative now than ever.

IV

If the only previous critical support for such a radical reappraisal of Shakespeare's timeless universality could be found in a handful of quotations from Coleridge and Hazlitt, compelling though their contentions are, it might well be objected that their corroboration simply confirms the antiquated nature of the whole concept, and the pointlessness of striving to breathe new life into terms ditched decades ago as tainted or defunct by most academics. But one need reach no further back than Robert Weimann's groundbreaking book *Shakespeare and the Popular Tradition in the Theater*, published in 1978, for corroboration from a more recent and quite different critical quarter. Weimann's classic Marxist study pulled the popular dimension of Shakespeare's drama and its theatrical roots into clear focus for the first time, revealing its anchorage not only in his spatial exploitation of the platform stage and its intimate relationship with the audience, but also in the language, form and structure of the plays. The pervasive influence of Weimann's book on Shakespearean scholarship and criticism is apparent in almost every subsequent study that deals with the dramatist's stagecraft, the interplay of actor, role and audience, or the perspective and discourse of plebeian characters and especially clowns and fools.

The punchline of Weimann's argument, however, was plainly found unpalatable, even by its most enthusiastic admirers in the Anglophone academic community, and was consequently filtered out of the book's reception as the unsavoury residue of an outmoded critical discourse. The final paragraph of the book concludes that the result of Shakespeare's bringing a plethora of conflicting viewpoints into dynamic, open-ended dialogue with each other within the bounds of a single play was a dramatic vision 'as broad as the newly universal vision of ideas and relationships within postfeudal society':

> If the poet, as I have suggested, could dramatically juxtapose and evaluate the ideals or attitudes of both service and individualism, honor and property, sophistication and simplicity, cynicism and naivety, these attitudes were useful in dramatic composition precisely because the resulting tensions were not blurred but transformed into tragic conflict or comic incongruity. Shakespeare was in a position to do this because he possessed, as a touchstone to test his material, a standpoint more freely, more critically, more richly apprehended than the particular social attitude or moral concept in question. Shakespeare's universal vision of experience was so secure and remained essentially unshaken because he had access to the fully developed techniques and values of a popular theater turned into a national institution. Amidst the 'mingle-mangle' of late Tudor and early Jacobean society these techniques helped to define and achieve a social and artistic position more

comprehensive and more vital in the areas of both its independence and its relatedness, its scepticism and its freedom.

This more comprehensive and vital social and artistic standpoint creates what Weimann has no qualms about calling, in the penultimate sentence of his study, 'the universalizing pattern in Shakespeare' and 'the humanizing quality of his achievement'.

Furthermore, the book's 'Appendix: Laughing with the Audience', a short, supplementary essay on the way Shakespearean comedy solicits from its audience 'the laughter of solidarity rather than that of satire', concludes by linking that drive to universalize and humanize to the adumbration of an authentic form of community beyond the purview of the present, but rooted in the tension between actual and potential, between what has been and what could be, that Hazlitt sensed in the plays. 'Shakespeare's comedy', Weimann contends in his closing sentence,

> points to a state of society, or, more likely, to a vision of Utopia that precludes any *Entzweiung* or alienation between the self and the social. The function and the structure of the genre are most deeply affected by some of the past echoes and future perspectives which, in Shakespeare's time, were possible in the context of the Renaissance reception and transmutation of the popular tradition in the theater.

In sharp contrast, however, to conservative critical versions of Shakespeare's universality and consequent transcendence of his age, Weimann's version is inseparable from the plays' entrenchment in their world and time: 'The universalizing pattern in Shakespeare and the "myriad-mindedness" of his art were never outside history, but they lived beyond the historical conditions that made them possible.' They did so thanks not least to 'The profound interaction of poetic imagination and theatrical technique' in the plays, which involved the interaction of actors and spectators, 'all participating in a common cultural and social activity' that united them, if only for the 'two hours' traffic of our stage', at a level inconceivable in everyday life beyond the licensed space of the public theatre. 'The interplay of poetry and theater itself', in other words, 'helps to constitute the universalizing pattern of Shakespeare's drama.' That pattern is not, therefore, inherent in the narrative facts of the plays – an ageless human plight clothed in the fleeting contingencies of a particular culture – but a consequence of the ways in which, and the perspective from which, the plays are fashioned and phrased by the dramatist and apprehended by the audience.

In this respect, Weimann's contention converges with Hazlitt's conviction that 'The striking peculiarity of Shakspeare's mind was its generic quality, its power of communication with all other minds – so that it contained a universe of thought and feeling within itself, and had no one peculiar bias, or exclusive excellence more than another.' It's not that Shakespeare looks at life in his time through the lens of his sources, and sees the timeless human story enduring beneath the illusion of historical development and social transformation; it's rather that he looks at the intransigent social reality of his moment in history, refracted through other tales and transmuted by his own dramatic art, from a universal human point of view that is bound, but not confined, to his time. Thus, when Weimann describes 'the universalizing and humanizing effect of Shakespeare's dramaturgy within a play world and upon a real world beset alike by rigid class barriers', he's not suggesting that the universalizing effect of Shakespeare's dramaturgy is to remove those barriers by some theatrical or poetical sleight of hand. On the contrary, those rigid barriers remain oppressively in place, both within the play for the characters and in the real world for the audience when they leave the theatre. How could it be otherwise? But if the performance of the play has been effective, Weimann implies, they should leave the theatre in possession of a perspective on the real world which transforms their perception of it.

The main problem with the punchline of Weimann's argument, and the reason why it failed to persuade radically inclined critics to take the concept of Shakespeare's universality seriously, was that it remained stranded at the level of abstract assertion, and thus incapable of grounding its argument in close analysis of the language and form of particular plays. One aim of this book is therefore to pick up where *Shakespeare and the Popular Tradition in the Theater* left off, provide a cogent rationale and textual support for its conclusion, and in so doing demonstrate the full significance and the importance of recognizing 'the universalizing pattern in Shakespeare' and 'the humanizing quality of his achievement'. The recognition that 'the universalizing and humanizing effect of Shakespeare's dramaturgy' is the source of its timeless quality remains equally embryonic and undeveloped in Weimann's book, but can be inferred from his assertion that Shakespearean comedy 'points to a state of society, or, more likely, to a vision of Utopia that precludes any *Entzweiung* or alienation between the self and the social'; from his perception that it is as 'deeply affected' by 'future perspectives' as by 'past echoes'; and above all from his insistence that 'The universalizing pattern in Shakespeare and the "myriad-mindedness" of his art were never outside history, but they lived beyond the historical conditions that made them possible' thanks to his poetic and theatrical transmutation of his material.

For a theoretical warrant that elucidates the link between universality and timelessness in art in terms that bring us closer to understanding their distinctive synergy in Shakespeare we need to turn to a thinker in the same utopian Marxist tradition as Weimann – the tradition that reaches back through the Frankfurt School and through Marx himself to Goethe, whose politically progressive concept of 'a universal world literature', serving the common human interests that transect divisive conventions and cultural differences, possessed a ready-made touchstone in Shakespeare. In his last book, *The Aesthetic Dimension*, published in the same year as *Shakespeare and the*

Popular Tradition in the Theater, Herbert Marcuse submits the following thesis:

> the radical qualities of art, that is to say, its indictment of the established reality and its invocation of the beautiful image (*schöner Schein*) of liberation are grounded precisely in the dimensions where art *transcends* its social determination and emancipates itself from the given universe of discourse and behaviour while preserving its overwhelming presence. Thereby art creates the realm in which the subversion of experience proper to art becomes possible: the world formed by art is recognized as a reality which is suppressed and distorted in the given reality. This experience culminates in extreme situations (of love and death, guilt and failure, but also joy, happiness, and fulfilment) which explode the given reality in the name of a truth normally denied or even unheard. The inner logic of the work of art terminates in the emergence of another reason, another sensibility, which defy the rationality and sensibility incorporated in the dominant social institutions.

It's vital to note how careful Marcuse is to stress that authentic art *transcends* its social determination but does not escape it. On the contrary, it *preserves* the 'overwhelming presence' of 'the given universe of discourse and behaviour' from which it emancipates itself. Its subversive defiance of 'the rationality and sensibility incorporated in the dominant social institutions' in the name of an alternative reality does not dispose of the prevailing historical reality in which their dominion must be endured. But through that defiance and transcendence, art at its most powerful is capable of creating in the reader, viewer or auditor, what Marcuse calls a 'rebellious subjectivity', whose 'indictment of the established reality' is inseparable from an awareness of the possibility of humanity's liberation from the established reality.

The secret of great art's capacity to do this, according to Marcuse, lies not in *what* it represents but in *how* it represents it: 'The critical function of art, its contribution to the struggle for liberation, resides in the aesthetic form.' The subject matter of the work in question is secondary to the specific ways in which it is shaped and transfigured, because

> Inasmuch as man and nature are constituted by an unfree society, their repressed and distorted potentialities can be represented only in an *estranging* form. The world of art is that of another *Reality Principle*, of estrangement – and only as estrangement does art fulfil a *cognitive* function: it communicates truths not communicable in any other language ... The encounter with the truth of art happens in the estranging language and images which make perceptible, visible and audible that which is no longer, or not yet, perceived, said, and heard in everyday life.

Through the 'aesthetic stylization' of the everyday life of its time art reveals the 'repressed and distorted potentialities' of the 'unfree society' from which it springs. Those potentialities are by definition the common possession of humanity rather than the property of a particular class, society, race or gender. Their revelation through 'the estranging language and images' of art is thus what endows art with its universal quality, with its ability to speak in the interests of humanity as a whole rather than in the interests of one section of humanity at the expense of the rest; to speak what Marcuse means by 'truth', in other words, instead of mouthing the lies of ideology: 'The universality of art cannot be grounded in the world and world outlook of a particular class, for art envisions a concrete universal, humanity (*Menschlichkeit*), which no particular class can incorporate, not even the proletariat, Marx's "universal class".'

The transmutation wrought by the alchemy of aesthetic form projects the vision of art beyond the dehumanized reality of social, sexual and racial inequality, which it invites us to view from the virtual vantage point of a humanity liberated from the alienation, injustice and oppression it has inflicted, and continues to inflict, on itself. Insofar as art that deserves the name of art is capable of creating any kind of 'collective consciousness', Marcuse maintains, 'it is that of individuals united in their awareness of the universal need for liberation – regardless of their class position. Nietzsche's *Zarathustra* dedication "Für Alle und Keinen" (For All and None) may apply also to the truth of art.' Because of the intellectual contempt with which the idea of art's universality is routinely regarded, not just by most Shakespearean academics but also in academic literary enclaves at large, it's essential to emphasize that what Marcuse has in mind when he invokes the idea is not art's expression of some underlying, immutable domain of human experience beyond the reach of history. He means that art achieves universality insofar as its representation of historical reality is predicated on, and committed to, 'The emergence of human beings as "species beings" – men and women capable of living in that community of freedom which is the potential of the species.' The realization of that potential, moreover, 'presupposes a radical transformation of the drives and needs of individuals' that may justifiably be termed revolutionary. For in 'the aesthetically most perfect works', as Marcuse puts it, 'the necessity of revolution is presupposed as the *a priori* of art'.

This concept of universality in art is the absolute antithesis of the concept as it is understood by both conservative critics and the radical critics who view its ascription to literature as reactionary and obsolete. Far from dissolving history, it is derived from and depends on it; far from precluding or denying the possibility of progressive social change, it demands nothing less than revolution to satisfy the true needs and full potential of human beings. The universal work of art for Marcuse is 'timeless' in the sense that it depicts an aspect or a version of life in its time in the terms of its time, *but not from the standpoint of its time*. In other words, it steps out of the history in which it is steeped in order to view life through the alien eyes of an anticipated era, in which past possibilities have blossomed at last into present realities.

'The possible "other" which appears in art is transhistorical', Marcuse explains, 'inasmuch as it transcends any and every specific historical situation', propelled by 'the principle of increasing the human potential for happiness'; and therein lies 'the perhaps most powerful kinship between art and revolution'. Art can transcend its specific historical situation, however, only through an imaginative representation of the prevailing reality from the viewpoint of the universal human interests which that reality betrays. For through the aesthetic process of representation 'mimesis translates reality into memory. In this remembrance, art has recognized what is and what could be, within and beyond social conditions.' On this understanding, the plays of Shakespeare can be seen as memories of the future *par excellence*, which translate the present they originally dramatized into the distant past of the desirable world they prefigure. To highlight the utopian dimension of Shakespeare's drama is not to dispute or repress its indelible historicity. On the contrary: the plays' universality is the product of the specific historical situation they transcend; their visionary utopianism is indivisible from their imaginative realism, from the depth and detail in which they dramatize life in Shakespeare's time. In this respect they provide perfect illustrations of the point with which Marcuse draws the argument of *The Aesthetic Dimension* to its conclusion:

> The *nomos* which art obeys is not that of the established reality principle but of its negation. But mere negation would be abstract, the 'bad' utopia. The utopia in great art is never the simple negation of the reality principle but its transcending preservation [*Aufhebung*] in which past and present cast their shadow on fulfilment. The authentic utopia is grounded in recollection.

Marcuse's closing qualification is crucial for understanding what I call the *utopian realism* of Shakespeare's dramatic art, and thus understanding why a fundamental reappraisal of its claim to universality and timelessness matters so much today.

The hostility such a reappraisal is prone to attract from *bien-pensant* Shakespeareans – a hostility commonly buttressed by a wilful misunderstanding of the argument – makes it important to labour the point already made. Shakespeare's plays *preserve* the historical reality that they transcend by virtue of their universalizing perspective, which gains its credibility and its power precisely from that preservation. In Marcuse's terms, the past and the present cast their shadows on the prospect of fulfilment illuminated by the plays. Shakespeare's drama is authentically utopian – as opposed to utopian in the pejorative sense of absurdly unrealistic and implausible – insofar as it is grounded in the recollection of Shakespeare's world and time. In this poetically encoded act of remembrance, to quote Marcuse's words again, the dramatic art of Shakespeare 'has recognized what is and what could be, within and beyond social conditions'.

To read, study, teach and perform Shakespeare's drama today on this assumption would be to activate the authentic utopian vision it harbours, a vision that reaches beyond the social conditions of the present age too. A truly historical study of Shakespeare's plays – unlike the arid antiquarianism that has stultified students of them in recent decades – would approach them not only as documents of their day, but also as dispatches from alternative futures, whose possibility they were *historically* empowered to disclose through their estranged dramatization of Shakespeare's times. It would free Shakespeare's drama to remind us, in words and deeds first staged four centuries ago, that – to quote the final sentences of *The Aesthetic Dimension*: 'The horizon of history is still open. If the remembrance of things past would become a motive in the struggle for changing the world, the struggle would be waged for a revolution hitherto suppressed in the previous historical revolutions.'

To enable Shakespeare's remembrance of things past to become a motive in this struggle today, it's vital to activate the anticipatory impetus of his drama, which keeps it out of sync with its time, and which renders the past-bound historicism of the academy incapable of accounting for its perpetual modernity. In the next chapter, therefore, I want to consider in more detail this untimely, anachronistic aspect of Shakespeare's art and its part in making him appear 'as unlike his cotemporaries as he is unlike us'. I'll then go on to show more precisely in Chapter 3 how the plays' transcendence of the times they dramatize, and hence their fabled timeless quality, spring from their universalizing commitment to the cause of humanity as a whole.

CHAPTER TWO

'Prophecies/Of this our Time'

I

In *Dr Copernicus*, John Banville's marvellous novel about another titan of the early modern era, the global impact of whose work is also still being felt today, Copernicus's disciple Joachim von Lauchen, the man responsible for the publication of *De Revolutionibus Orbium Coelestium*, delivers this striking confession of his personal creed:

> I was then, and I am still, despite my loss of faith, one of those who look to the future for redemption, I mean redemption from the world, which has nothing to do with Christ's outlandish promises, but with the genius of Man. ... Yes, I look to the future, live in the future, and so, when I speak of the present, I am as it were looking backward, into what is, for me, already the past. Do you follow that?

Shakespeare, I'm quite sure, would have had no trouble following that, since it resonates so strongly with his own vision. That he knew what it meant to live imaginatively in the future while speaking of the present in which mere chance has obliged one to dwell can be readily inferred from much of his poetry and most of his plays. It was a creative cast of mind so deeply ingrained in him that, at its most developed, it allowed Shakespeare to dramatize the present, in various guises, as if it were indeed already the past; to dramatize it, grammatically speaking, in the future perfect, as the way things *will have been*, as the way his world might one day seem to citizens of more civilized centuries to come.

For explicit evidence of Shakespeare's proleptic imagination at work we don't have to look far. In the *Sonnets* we find poem after poem projecting itself into the future, anticipating some subjunctive scenario and turning it into a prophecy of what will come to pass long after its author's demise, as in the uncannily prescient final quatrain and couplet of Sonnet 81:

> Your monument shall be my gentle verse,
> Which eyes not yet created shall o'er-read,
> And tongues to be your being shall rehearse
> When all the breathers of this world are dead.
> > You still shall live – such virtue hath my pen –
> > Where breath most breathes, even in the mouths of men.

To read these lines aloud now, to resurrect the beloved youth by rehearsing his being once more, is to become the envisaged possessors of the 'eyes not yet created', the 'tongues to be', whom their author predicted would be reading them long after he, and everyone alive at the moment he penned them, had ceased to exist. Moreover, as we speak the line 'When all the breathers of this world are dead' today, the poem folds us into its posthumous embrace, foreshadowing the time when we too, together with everyone still breathing now, will have passed away, while the sonnet survives us, kept alive 'Where breath most breathes, even in the mouths of men' whom we shall never know.

Shakespeare seems to have had little doubt that the events he was dramatizing and the words he was writing were destined to echo on through the centuries in countries that did not even exist yet and in languages of which he had never heard, as the rhetorical question Cassius poses, as he stands over Caesar's lacerated corpse, suggests:

> How many ages hence
> Shall this our lofty scene be acted over,
> In states unborn and accents yet unknown?
>
> (3.1.112–14)

The rhetorical question Brutus poses immediately after this is less familiar:

> How many times shall Caesar bleed in sport,
> That now on Pompey's basis lies along,
> No worthier than the dust?
>
> (3.1.115–17)

But it's equally important to quote it, because these lines link the urge to vault forward into the future with the desire to lay the mighty low, to make them equal with the dust in which they must be laid with the poor crooked scythe and spade. The same flash of precognition, coupled with the same drive to debase, is apparent in Cleopatra's prophecy of the theatrical afterlife she and Antony are fated to share:

> The quick comedians
> Extemporally will stage us, and present
> Our Alexandrian revels. Antony
> Shall be brought drunken forth, and I shall see
> Some squeaking Cleopatra boy my greatness
> I'th' posture of a whore.
>
> (5.2.212–17)

Latter-day audiences hearing these lines hear lines deliberately designed, like Cassius's, to be heard by them, as they watch the 'quick comedians' of our age stage the play, as well as by the tragedy's earliest audiences, who would have heard them declaimed in the 'squeaking' voice of the 'boy' cross-dressed as Cleopatra, and thus witnessed a prediction being made in ancient Alexandria being fulfilled in Jacobean London.

Like the prospect of Caesar perennially bleeding 'in sport', as the 'lofty scene' of his assassination is reenacted on countless stages for the amusement of future audiences, the prospect of Antony and Cleopatra's tragic fate being travestied on the popular stage is tied to the pleasure it affords the spectators of seeing the powerful cut down to size. It's worth noting that the power to cut the powerful down to size is vested by Cleopatra in the actors, whose lethal gift for debunking the once dreaded by playing them, and by placing them at the mercy of their 'quick' extemporal wits, is foremost amongst the fears of 'a queen / Worth many babes and beggars' (5.2.46–7). It's also worth pausing over Shakespeare's pointed use of the adverb 'extemporally' in this context to describe the way in which 'The triple pillar of the world' (1.1.12) and the 'Sovereign of Egypt' (1.5.34) will be staged by the 'quick comedians' in order to degrade them.

The word means primarily here 'in an impromptu, impro-vised manner' and implies a resort to off-the-cuff quips at the immortal lovers' expense. But the word's Latin root lies closer to the surface at this point in the history of its usage, and the play's overt preoccupation with the lovers' metamorphosis into timeless creatures of myth brings it closer still. To speak or act *ex tempore* is to speak or act *out of time*: to skip the script and wing it, to talk out of turn by ad-libbing – as Shakespeare's wise fools, saucy servants and witty heroines habitually do – is to deviate from the scheduled succession of plot-bound events and exchanges, and thus to slip surreptitiously out of the clutches of clock-time into a timescape that defies calibration and chroni-cling. The sentence 'The quick comedians / Extemporally will stage us', whose phrasing and rhythm amplify 'Extemporally', entails an understanding of drama's capacity to transpose characters, deeds and speech derived from historical reality into this temporally unshackled domain by transforming it into 'sport', into a pastime for audiences already freed from quotidian chronology by entering the playtime of the theatre.

It points to a fundamental feature of Shakespeare's drama to which I've already adverted and to which I'll return: its ability to dramatize the temporal realm of history from an extemporal point of view. That point of view is *timeless* not because it perceives an underlying human condition that will always be the same, but because it's rooted in human potentiality rather than historical reality and its time has not yet come.

The extemporal perspective is produced, moreover, as Cleopatra's speech implies, by an act of theatrical mimesis: the actors will 'stage' Antony and Cleopatra and 'present' their 'Alexandrian revels', estranging them from their original selves and actual experience and transmuting them through travesty – in Cleopatra's case through the literal travesty of a transvestite, pubescent actor mimicking the mature female voice. The Queen of Egypt fears the actor's power to 'boy [her] greatness / I'th' posture of a whore'. The dramatic technique of extemporal estrangement is inseparable in this speech from the desire to humble the exalted, which is the expression in turn of the egalitarian standpoint from which the speech, like the whole tragedy of *Antony and Cleopatra*, was instinctively conceived and composed.

The same standpoint prompts the iconoclastic flight of fancy with which Hamlet concludes his extemporal bout of badinage with the gravedigger in the breathing-space Shakespeare grants him before the catastrophe. 'To what base uses we may return, Horatio!', exclaims Hamlet as he tosses Yorick's putrid skull back into the earth. 'Why may not imagination trace the noble dust of Alexander till a find it stopping a bung-hole?' (5.1.198–200). And he wraps the point up in a couple of wry couplets:

Imperial Caesar, dead and turned to clay,
Might stop a hole to keep the wind away.
O, that that earth which kept the world in awe
Should patch a wall t'expel the winter's flaw!
But soft, but soft; aside. Here comes the King ...

(5.5.208–12)

The echo of the speeches of Cassius and Brutus quoted above is unmissable and perhaps unsurprising, given their source in the tragedy Shakespeare penned immediately before *Hamlet*. Unlike Cleopatra, however, Hamlet, who has a soft spot for 'the quick comedians', and who scripts and stages a mousetrap for majesty, is not appalled but edified by the thought of greatness mocked and degraded, in this case by the indiscriminate Dance of Death. The immediate juxtaposition of that thought with the entry of the living king ensures that its direct bearing on the killer of Hamlet's father and the seducer of his mother, and the further warrant it supplies for dispatching him despite his royalty, are not lost on the audience.

That such contemptuous disenchantment with sovereignty and the baseless awe in which it expects to be held by the world should be placed in the mouth of a prince makes it all the more potent. It also confirms Hamlet's possession at this point of a vision as declutched from what passes for normality as the vision of the tragedy whose protagonist he is doomed to play. The faculty that makes that vision possible for Hamlet and his creator is the imagination, which enables the disaffected prince to 'trace the noble dust of Alexander till a find it stopping a bung-hole' and, by imagining the way the world wags from a different angle, turn the accepted view of the world upside down. The last line quoted, 'But soft, but soft; aside. Here comes the King', encapsulates the speaker's alienation from the entire regime incarnate in Claudius; it brackets the digressive discourse that precedes it as an extraneous interlude, a protracted departure from the business of the plot proper, whose resumption is announced by 'Here comes the King'; and, through Hamlet's use of the term 'aside' to signal that he and Horatio should now stand and speak apart, it glances at the key role played by staging, by theatrical performance, in framing a virtual time and space that power cannot police.

II

It's no accident, of course, that Hamlet's levelling reflections
are occasioned by his encounter with a gravedigger plying
his trade among the skeletal remains of the 'great folk'
(5.1.270) who once owned and ruled Denmark – the lords,
ladies, courtiers, politicians, lawyers and buyers of land to
whom, Hamlet fancies, the skulls tossed up by the gravedigger's spade might well belong. A setting more favourable to
fostering a posthumous perspective on the present would be
hard to imagine. That radically detached perspective governs
the sonnets obsessed with time and immortality too, a point
perfectly illustrated by Sonnet 81's envisagement of its being
read 'When all the breathers of this world are dead'. The
conclusion of Sonnet 81 reweaves the conclusion of Sonnet
18, employing virtually the same words to voice the same idea:
'So long as men can breathe or eyes can see, / So long lives this,
and this gives life to thee.' The opening of Sonnet 81 – 'Or I
shall live your epitaph to make, / Or you survive when I in
earth am rotten' – recycles likewise the more intimate confrontation of earlier sonnets with the prospect of the poet's or the
adored aristocratic youth's demise. Sonnet 32, for instance,
commences 'If thou survive my well-contented day / When
that churl death my bones with dust shall cover', and specu-
lates on the thoughts that might run through his inamorato's
mind, should he chance to 'once more resurvey / These poor
rude lines of [his] deceased lover' and compare them with the
lines penned by technically more accomplished poets 'since
he died'.

Shakespeare returns compulsively to envisioning his poetry
being read after his death in Sonnet 71 ('No longer mourn for
me when I am dead'), where he writes, 'O, if, I say, you look
upon this verse / When I perhaps compounded am with clay';
and in Sonnet 74, which invites the addressee to imagine the
moment 'When thou reviewest this' in the wake of its author's
extinction ('when that fell arrest / Without all bail shall carry

me away'). The proleptic attitude of these poems is epitomized by the preposition 'against', which they frequently employ as shorthand for 'in anticipation of'. Take, for instance, Sonnet 13's grim admonition to the beloved: 'Against this coming end you should prepare / ... Against the stormy gusts of winter's day, / And barren rage of death's eternal cold'; or the phrase that kicks off each quatrain of Sonnet 49 ('Against that time – if ever that time come – '); or the line that opens Sonnet 63, which deserves quotation in full for the barely disguised animus it betrays towards the object of the poet's adulation:

> Against my love shall be as I am now,
> With time's injurious hand crushed and o'erworn;
> When hours have drained his blood and filled his brow
> With lines and wrinkles; when his youthful morn
> Hath travelled on to age's steepy night,
> And all those beauties whereof now he's king
> Are vanishing, or vanished out of sight,
> Stealing away the treasure of his spring:
> For such a time do I now fortify
> Against confounding age's cruel knife,
> That he shall never cut from memory
> My sweet love's beauty, though my lover's life.
>   His beauty shall in these black lines be seen,
>   And they shall live, and he in them still green.

Despite being for the most part couched shrewdly in the third person rather than pitched as an apostrophe of the loved one, and despite being sealed with a couplet reassuring the latter yet again of its power to confer immortality on him, the sonnet fails to mask the vindictive violence lurking beneath its obsequious posture. The supposition that furnishes the poem's premise and generates the figurative diction of its quatrains is ostensibly innocuous, purporting as it does to describe the devastation 'time's injurious hand' has already wrought in the appearance of the ageing poet. But by fast-forwarding us to the remorseless day when 'my love shall be as I am now', the sonnet forges a pretext for its main purpose, which is to paint a merciless portrait of the beautiful youth butchered by 'confounding age's cruel knife'. After the first line the poet's rhetorical alibi, that he's describing his own current plight, recedes behind a sustained third-person projection of the havoc the future will wreak on the poet's aloof aristocratic lover as well.

The glaring difference in rank that divides them is as important to bear in mind while reading the poem as the painful disparity between their ages. One need only glance back at Sonnet 57, in which the poet casts himself as the abject 'sad slave' of the young man he addresses as 'my sovereign', or Sonnet 58, where he adopts the equally servile role of a 'vassal' at the beck and call of his feudal lord, to be reminded of how acutely aware the poet is of the gulf divorcing his low-born love from his high-born lover. With that gulf in mind, the punitive impulse behind the visualization of the youthful lord physically violated by the passing years reveals an ulterior motive socially rooted in *ressentiment*. When the 'sweet love's' superior rank breaks the sonnet's surface in the phrase 'all those beauties whereof now he's king', a vengeful regicidal subplot becomes apparent in the poem too. Its noble victim has been 'crushed' by an 'injurious hand' and his blood 'drained' from him; all that he was 'king' of has 'vanished' and his 'treasure' has been stolen; the poet's loyal resolve to 'fortify' his idol's beauty against oblivion with rhyme is helpless to save his 'lover's life' from being 'cut from memory' by the killer's 'cruel knife'.

Accentuating this aspect of the sonnet confirms the poet's imaginative complicity with 'time's injurious hand' in not just prematurely aging the idolized aristocrat but cutting him down in his prime. 'Against my love shall be as I am now': the base-born poet gets emotionally even with his *prince lointain* by concocting a scenario in which the passage of time has put them on equal terms by making them look and feel the same. Not content, however, with evening the odds between them by stressing their shared subjection to senescence and death, the

poet proceeds, as he does in so many of the sonnets, to invert
their hierarchical relationship by placing the young nobleman
at the mercy of his immortalizing verse. If that seems to be
reading too much into an ingenuous declaration of undying
devotion, corroboration of the attitude that animates the
subtext of Sonnet 63 can be found in the very next sonnet:

> When I have seen by time's fell hand defaced
> The rich proud cost of outworn buried age;
> When sometime-lofty towers I see down razed,
> And brass eternal slave to mortal rage;
> When I have seen the hungry ocean gain
> Advantage on the kingdom of the shore,
> And the firm soil win of the wat'ry main,
> Increasing store with loss and loss with store;
> When I have seen such interchange of state,
> Or state itself confounded to decay,
> Ruin hath taught me thus to ruminate:
> That time will come and take my love away.

The conclusion drawn in the last line quoted, and the couplet's
routine reflection upon it ('This thought is as a death, which
cannot choose / But weep to have that which it fears to lose')
are eclipsed by the meditation on the transience of privilege,
wealth and power in the preceding eleven lines, for which the
final three function merely as a retrospective pretext.

In Sonnet 64, what was overtly personal and covertly
political in Sonnet 63 becomes frankly political, as the
focus switches from the poet's patrician lover to any dispensation of the kind that men of his rank were born to rule.
The poem begins by contemplating the inexorable fate that
awaits the highest and mightiest in the land and the imposing
edifices erected by those who possess and preside to cow the
dispossessed and powerless. Ostentatious tombs designed
to trumpet the grandeur and wealth of their occupants to
posterity ('The rich proud cost of outworn buried age') are
doomed to wind up 'by time's fell hand defaced' as surely

as the 'sometime-lofty towers', which once proclaimed their owners' affluence and eminence, have wound up 'razed'. It's important to note that the sonnet is not musing indiscriminately on the 'sad mortality' (Sonnet 65) of all mankind any more than Hamlet is, when he muses on the putative owners of the skulls turfed up by the gravedigger; in neither case is Shakespeare defaulting to a predictable *memento mori* or *ubi sunt* motif. The sonnet is specifically concerned here, like Hamlet, with the fate that awaits those – including the poet's lover – whom the gravedigger calls 'great folk': the fate that makes a mockery of the greatness they preened themselves on while alive. The iconoclastic cue provided by the first quatrain prompts the image of insurrection latent in the language of the second's first two lines, in which a glimpse can be caught of a starving populace winning ground as it storms the seat of majesty: 'When I have seen the hungry ocean gain / Advantage on the kingdom of the shore'. And in the first two lines of the third quatrain the sonnet's insurgent imagery culminates in the prophetic recollection of 'such interchange of state, / Or state itself confounded to decay' – lines which share with Cassius's envisaging of 'states unborn' a profound grasp of the impermanence of the status quo. It's a realization which Shakespeare invites the poem's readers to share, too, by looking back with him in the aftermath of upheaval and ruination, and finding in the past a prognosis of what history holds in store for sovereigns and their satraps and all that they call theirs.

The insubordinate stand this sonnet takes on hierarchy is equally obvious in Sonnet 55, which pits the poem's assured longevity against those enthroned above the rest of their fellow human beings: 'Not marble nor the gilded monuments / Of princes shall outlive this powerful rhyme'. That defiant opening, with its emphatic iambic stress on 'princes', engenders thoughts of the further devastation yet to be wrought by 'wasteful war' at the implicit behest of princes, including the toppling of 'statues' that exalt pillars of the class in whose interest wars are waged. The sonnet derives its confidence in its superiority to the princes whose power its 'powerful rhyme' usurps from its adoption of the ultimate posthumous point of view: 'your praise shall still find room / Even in the eyes of all posterity / That wear this world out to the ending doom.' The gravedigger, who easily bests Prince Hamlet in their battle of wits, catapults us forward to the same apocalyptic vanishing point, immediately before the royal protagonist enters the tragedy's last act, when he extols the plebeian prowess of the grave-maker, because 'the houses that he makes lasts till doomsday' (5.1.59). Gazing back upon the ruins of human history at the end of time, after the war-torn world of princes has worn itself out, the poet arrogates to himself the divine omnipotence to which the absolute rulers of his world laid claim in vain.

Further confirmation of this cast of mind is furnished by Sonnet 107, whose couplet puts the contempt its author feels for oppressive autocrats beyond dispute: 'And thou in this shalt find thy monument / When tyrants' crests and tombs of brass are spent.' The poet's animus is directed quite specifically here at despotic rulers, and he prides himself on the fact that his verse will outlive not only them, but also, as in sonnets 63 and 64, the entire class to which the man he professes to worship belongs, the man who will regard him after his death, he tells him, as 'Too base by thee to be rememberèd' (Sonnet 74). The couplet in which Sonnet 107 culminates has an oracular ring, moreover, which befits a poem suffused with the spirit of prognostication, from its opening invocation of 'the prophetic soul / Of the wide world dreaming on things to come' to its report that 'the sad augurs mock their own presage' while 'peace proclaims olives of endless age'. The dream of 'things to come' is the global dream of humanity, the universal dream that the whole 'wide world' is dreaming; indeed, prophetic dreaming is so fundamental to the world, Shakespeare implies, as to spring from, if not constitute, its very 'soul'. (It's apt, perhaps, to recall here Jonson's apostrophe of Shakespeare as the 'Soul of the age'.) From the juxtaposition of this opening image of global humanity 'dreaming on things to come' with the couplet's anticipation of a time when all the tyrants of the world will have perished, the poem's readers may be left to draw their own conclusions about its author's allegiances.

Circling back to Sonnet 81 with this sonnet and the other sonnets I've cited in mind, the nature of those allegiances becomes even plainer. Shakespeare's capacity to imagine himself, as he does in Sonnet 74, 'The prey of worms, my body being dead', is paradoxically empowering: viewing things from beyond the grave frees him to adopt a stance of prescient retrospection, to think in the future perfect, as if he were already detached from a self and a society, from a whole way of life, which he had left far behind, and could contemplate from the vantage point of the end of the world. I want to say more in the last chapter of this book about the posthumous perspective, which informs so much of Shakespeare's drama and poetry, even when – perhaps especially when – its adoption is not apparent. At this point I just want to stress how inseparable that perspective is from the dream of equality, and from the transcendence of time, in the mind of the man who wrote the *Sonnets*.

In the second quatrain of Sonnet 81 he writes:

Your name from hence immortal life shall have,
Though I, once gone, to all the world must die.
The earth can yield me but a common grave
When you entombèd in men's eyes shall lie.

The poet 'to all the world must die': his post-mortem detachment from the living will be complete, although its global scale lends his deceased self a poignant grandeur, which offsets the oblivion to which he affects to consign it. Thanks to the poet, however, his aristocratic lover shall enjoy the 'immortal life' the sonnets guarantee him after his physical demise; his mortal remains will be interred in a splendid tomb suited to a man of his rank for the eyes of the living to admire, but only his figurative entombment in the eyes of future readers of these poems can grant him true immortality. The adroit inversion of hierarchy, masquerading as self-deprecation, is a rhetorical ruse familiar from other sonnets: in the long run the poet will outrank the nobleman, to whom he is now socially subordinate, by virtue of his command of the language, reversing the roles that historical happenstance has assigned them. In the counterfactual realm of the poem, the extemporal realm unfettered by the concept of time that imprisons human beings in history, the poet whose birth permits him 'but a common grave' has the upper hand and the last word.

The word 'common' in this context undergoes a semantic transformation, as its derogatory connotations mutate into their opposite, making interment in 'a common grave' provided merely by 'The earth' the virtue of the poet, on whose base-born gift the noble youth's undying fame depends. The primary sense of 'common', dictated by its disparaging contrast with the youth's literal and metaphorical entombment 'in men's eyes', is 'undistinguished', 'ordinary', 'of the common people, the masses'; and in Shakespeare's time, when the bones of *hoi polloi* were routinely jumbled together in charnel houses, 'a common grave' might also designate a grave anonymously shared with others deemed to deserve no better fate. But the rhetorical argument of Sonnet 81 redeems the word 'common', activating the positive, levelling connotations it carries openly in other contexts, such as Timon's apostrophe of the earth, the same earth that will yield the poet 'but a common grave': 'Common mother – thou / Whose womb unmeasurable and infinite breast / Teems and feeds all' (4.3.178–80). The classless human perspective implicit in the image of the earth's common grave is the perspective of the posthumous future from which the sonnet was written in Shakespeare's intractably hierarchical world.

The first-person viewpoint of the *Sonnets*, refracted though it is through the poet's persona and the formal conventions of the sonnet, reveals how deeply ingrained this habit of preemptive hindsight was in Shakespeare's mind. Even at its most intensely intimate and emotionally charged, his writing instinctively reaches forward in order to turn back and behold in what has yet to be what will have come to pass.

So fundamental is utopian retrospection to the composition of the *Sonnets* that their author's egalitarian bent leaves its proleptic imprint on poems whose obsessions at first glance might seem purely personal.

III

To turn again from the *Sonnets* to the plays is to throw still more starkly into relief their constant endeavour to slip the shackles of 'this vile world' (Sonnet 71) that spawned them too, and dramatize its agonies and absurdities as if they belonged to the superseded past of a truly civilized world. Nowhere is the centrality of that endeavour to the vision of the plays more self-evident than in *King Lear*. At the turning point of the tragedy, as Kent leads the demented monarch off to shelter from the storm that has stripped away his royalty, the Fool hangs back, steps out of the world and time of the play, and addresses the audience directly in characteristically cryptic terms:

> This is a brave night to cool a courtesan. I'll speak a prophecy ere I go:
>> When priests are more in word than matter;
>> When brewers mar their malt with water;
>> When nobles are their tailors' tutors,
>> No heretics burned, but wenches' suitors,
>> Then shall the realm of Albion
>> Come to great confusion.
>
>> When every case in law is right;
>> No squire in debt nor no poor knight;
>> When slanders do not live in tongues,
>> Nor cutpurses come not to throngs;
>> When usurers tell their gold i'th' field,
>> And bawds and whores do churches build,

Then comes the time, who lives to see't,
That going shall be used with feet.
This prophecy Merlin shall make; for I live before his time.
(3.2.79–95)

'This is one of the Shakespearian shocks or blows that take
the breath away', remarked G. K. Chesterton of that extraordinary last line, struck like everyone who hears or reads it by
the sudden sense of temporal vertigo it induces.

Pitched between wry plebeian satire and self-mocking
parody, the Fool's vatic doggerel fuses harsh Jacobean realities
with millennial possibilities, deliberately dislocating our
temporal point of view. In a modern production, a twenty-
first-century audience is addressed by a mercurial figure in
an early modern drama about ancient Britain, who employs
mock-Chaucerian verse to make a prediction not due to be
delivered until the mythical reign of King Arthur several
centuries later. Past, future and present are scrambled to
confound our normal linear conception of time and place us,
for one dizzying moment, in an unknown future far ahead
of whatever age we live in too. The speech foregrounds the
complex anachronistic construction of *King Lear*, which uses
every ruse of estrangement to stay out of sync with its era.
The Fool, whose riddling prophecy encapsulates the larger
prophetic riddle of *King Lear*, personifies at this moment the
whole play's disruption of chronological time in the name of a
vision of history to which the prospect of transformation has
been restored.

As Walter Cohen notes in *Drama of a Nation*, taking his
cue from the Fool's prophecy, the prophecies of Merlin were
linked to radicalism in Shakespeare's day, and both before and
during the Civil War fools and madmen were associated with
revolutionary prophecy. In the 'handy-dandy' speeches to
Gloucester in Act 4, which appropriate the riddling discourse
of the Fool, the 'reason in madness' (4.5.171) that Lear utters
presages the views of the Levellers and even the more radical
beliefs of the Ranters and Diggers. 'Whatever the direct

influence of the play on the Revolution,' Cohen concludes, '*King Lear* takes its place in a tradition of popular radicalism ... that may extend without a break from the Peasants' Revolt of 1381 to the present.' In *Signifying Nothing* Malcolm Evans likewise draws a line linking *Lear*'s alignment with the dispossessed directly to the radical ideologies of the Revolution and the execution of 'the great image of authority' (4.5.154), Charles I, in 1649. He also recognizes the indeterminate time of the Fool's prophecy of a prophecy as central to the play's vision, finding in both the Fool's and the mad king's inverted logic 'a figure not only of "nothing" but also of the utopian plenitude associated with carnival and the Land of Cockaygne'.

The same battle between utopian possibility and dystopian reality is waged at the heart of Shakespeare's last masterpiece, *The Tempest*, whose equally apocalyptic world view crystallizes in its most famous speech. That battle is pulled into focus and ironically framed in the opening scene of Act 2, when Gonzalo's flight of fantasy to the Land of Cockaygne is grounded for a moment in mid-sentence by Sebastian's and Antonio's sarcastic interjections. 'Had I plantation of this isle, my lord', opines Gonzalo, 'And were the king on't',

> I'th' commonwealth I would by contraries
> Execute all things. For no kind of traffic
> Would I admit, no name of magistrate;
> Letters should not be known; riches, poverty,
> And use of service, none; contract, succession,
> Bourn, bound of land, tilth, vineyard, none;
> No use of metal, corn, or wine, or oil;
> No occupation, all men idle, all;
> And women too – but innocent and pure;
> No sovereignty –

Sebastian (*to Antonio*) Yet he would be king on't.

Antonio The latter end of his commonwealth forgets the beginning.

> (2.1.149, 151,153–64)

Those who share the cynical realism of Sebastian and Antonio are prone to forget the kind of men Shakespeare conscripts to ridicule 'the Golden Age' (2.1.174) Gonzalo envisions by pointing out the glaring contradiction on which it's founded. Their automatic assumption that such visions are inherently flawed and self-evidently futile also inclines them to forget the irrepressible momentum of Gonzalo's utopian prospectus, which runs on regardless of the cynical sniping until its panoramic survey of his ideal commonwealth is complete. Although the treacherous hecklers are allowed the last word, crying 'Save his majesty!' and 'Long live Gonzalo!' (2.1.174–5) to underscore the fatal flaw in the honest old councillor's reasoning, that flaw doesn't invalidate his utopian dream, only the premise on which it's based and the means by which it's to be achieved. The fact that Shakespeare drew directly for Gonzalo's speech on a passage in Montaigne's essay 'Of the Caniballes', in which Montaigne praises the 'perfection' of a society that puts Plato's 'imaginarie common-wealth' to shame, should suffice to give one pause before assuming that the intended effect of this episode is anti-utopian.

The chief target of Sebastian's and Antonio's derision, after all, is not the idyllic regime Gonzalo describes or its plausibility as such. It's the vanity Gonzalo unwittingly betrays in his fantasy of benign omnipotence, which blinds him to the contradiction between his wish to be king of the utopian colony he would create on the island and his knowledge that the essential precondition of a truly civilized society is 'No sovereignty'. Gonzalo is mocked because 'The latter end of his commonwealth forgets the beginning', not because the notion of a society free from tyranny, toil, war and the exploitation of the earth, where poverty is unknown because wealth is truly shared, and an undefiled nature produces 'All things in common' (2.1.165), is inherently preposterous. On the contrary, even Antonio's sneer that freedom from marriage and labour would make Gonzalo's subjects 'whores and knaves' (2.1.172), despite the latter's blinkered assurance that women would remain 'innocent and pure', hardly detracts from the positive appeal of Gonzalo's commonwealth as a whole, as Shakespeare, following Montaigne, portrays it. That particular features of that commonwealth are open to objection on modern or early modern grounds needs no further demonstration, its vulnerability to critique having been established by Shakespeare himself through Antonio and Sebastian. The main point of the entire exchange is irreducible, however, to the playwright's endorsement of either party at the expense of the other. Its main point is not that the creation of a genuine commonwealth of truly 'innocent people' (2.1.170) is impossible, but that the fundamental obstacle to its creation is sovereignty and the unequal distribution of property, wealth and power that sovereignty entails.

'For I am all the subjects that you have, / Which first was mine own king' (1.2.343–4), Caliban justly complains to the man who has stolen his island and enslaved him, having learned first-hand the hard way that sovereignty by definition demands and produces subjection. Not the least startling thing about *The Tempest*, as the critique of Gonzalo's utopia and Caliban's rebuke make clear, is the understanding it presupposes on the part of the playwright that there can be no true commonwealth as long as sovereignty exists. It's significant, moreover, that Gonzalo's interrupted line reads 'No sovereignty – ' rather than 'No sovereign – ', because 'sovereign' would risk restricting the reference historically to individual kings of the kind who ruled the absolute monarchies of Shakespeare's day, whereas 'sovereignty' denotes the possession of supreme authority and power as such, whatever form it takes in any society in any era. The line 'No sovereignty – ', amplified by its abrupt truncation, which lends it the force of a demand, puts the future-perfect standpoint from which the exchange was written beyond doubt, because it's predicated on the knowledge that sovereignty cannot solve the systemic problems of which it is the principal source.

Machiavelli's *The Prince*, Erasmus's *The Education of a Christian Prince*, Thomas Elyot's *The Boke Named the*

Governour, *The Mirror for Magistrates*: merely to cite the titles of such influential Renaissance 'mirrors for princes' is to be reminded that even for the more enlightened intellects of Shakespeare's age an actual society not governed by a sovereign power was inconceivable. Even Thomas More's fictional *Utopia* is premised on the assumption that the prototypical communist society it describes would have to be founded by sovereign fiat – in this case by King Utopus – and thus imposed from above rather than collectively forged from below by the people. Whether Shakespeare drew on More's *Utopia* in writing *The Tempest* may be a matter for dispute, but there's no disputing the fact that the man who wrote the dialogue between Gonzalo, Sebastian and Antonio about creating a true commonwealth was on the same wavelength as the man who wrote the conclusion drawn by Raphael Hythloday from the contrast between Utopia and the European reality to which he has returned:

> Therefore, when I consider and weigh in my mind all these commonwealths which nowadays anywhere do flourish, so God help me, I can perceive nothing but a certain conspiracy of rich men procuring their own commodities under the name and title of the commonwealth. They invent and devise all means and crafts, first how to keep safely without fear of losing that they have unjustly gathered together, and next how to hire and abuse the work and labour of the poor for as little money as may be. These devices, when the rich men have decreed to be kept and observed under colour of the commonalty, that is to say, also of the poor people, then they be made laws.
>
> But these wicked and vicious men, when they have by their insatiable covetousness divided among themselves all those things, which would have sufficed all men, yet how far be they from the wealth and felicity of the Utopian commonwealth?

The pertinence of this scathing indictment to our current

predicament scarcely needs spelling out. Its blunt truth is more glaringly apparent today, in the wake of the global financial crisis and the bailing out of the banks, than it was when More penned it half a millennium ago at the dawn of the capitalist era. To be sure, the only scathing thing about the dialogue between Gonzalo, Sebastian and Antonio in *The Tempest* is the mockery of the elder statesman's blueprint for a society that would 'excel the golden age' (2.1.166). To find Shakespeare skewering the same culprits in the same caustic vein one must turn back to *King Lear*:

> Through tattered clothes strong vices do appear;
> Robes and furred gowns hide all. Plate sin with gold,
> And the strong lance of justice hurtless breaks;
> Arm it in rags, a pygmy's straw does pierce it.
>
> (4.6.160–3)

But what makes the exchange in *The Tempest* resonate as powerfully with Hythloday's words as Lear's do is the authors' shared realization that no society can call itself a commonwealth unless its wealth and power are really held in common by its free and equal citizens, instead of hogged by the few who govern in their own interest 'under colour of the commonalty'.

'The latter end of his commonwealth forgets the beginning': the visionary anachronism of the imagination that forged that retort to Gonzalo's self-deluding boast 'No sovereignty –' is more radical, however, than the visionary anachronism of the imagination that dreamt up *Utopia* a century earlier. The fact that More was obliged to invent a benign royal dictator to explain the origin of his ideal commonwealth reveals the point at which his astonishing feat of the imagination ran up against the limits of what was historically imaginable. To put it simply, More would see no problem in Gonzalo's being the founder and king of his own utopian commonwealth. But for Shakespeare, writing a century after *Utopia*, it's the very existence of kings, indeed the idea of sovereignty as such, that is the fundamental problem preventing the creation of a true commonwealth. From Shakespeare's point of view the latter end of More's commonwealth forgets its beginning too, rendering his utopia a contradiction in terms.

It's not just in *King Lear* that one can discern a direct subterranean link to the English Revolution and the execution of 'the great image of authority' in the sovereign shape of Charles I a few decades after Shakespeare's death. The same subversive logic drives Caliban's defiant deconstruction of Prospero's authority over him. When Caliban declares, 'For I am all the subjects that you have, / Which first was mine own king', he collapses the distinction between sovereign and subject by invoking a time before such a distinction, and the oppressive power relations it involves, existed. Caliban's subjection to Prospero is neither natural nor inevitable, but a state the latter has inflicted on the former for his own benefit, and with Prospero's departure for Milan with the rest of the island's transient inhabitants, Caliban will be his own king once more, as the distinction between sovereign and subject dissolves. Myopic accounts of the dialogue between Gonzalo, Antonio and Sebastian that confine themselves to what's manifestly undesirable or defective about Gonzalo's commonwealth, or to the justified gibes it attracts from his cynical companions, miss the really remarkable thing about it, which is the fact that it's the product of an imagination light years ahead of its time and still way ahead of what most people find imaginable in ours. It's written, like the whole play whose vision it encapsulates, from a standpoint in a conceivable world beyond sovereignty and subjection, where 'all things' are executed 'by contraries', and life is thus the polar opposite of what it used to be.

The most compelling testimony to the radical detachment of *The Tempest*'s vision is furnished by the play's most quoted speech. Prospero's sudden recollection of 'that foul conspiracy / Of the beast Caliban and his confederates' (4.1.139–40) brings the betrothal masque to an abrupt end. At his terse behest, '*To a strange, hollow, and confused noise, the spirits in the pageant heavily vanish*'. 'This is strange', remarks Ferdinand, underlining the uncanny quality of the moment, as Prospero is seized by 'some passion' (4.1.143), whose source Ferdinand can't perceive. And the look of apparent dismay on the face of his daughter's fiancé elicits this response from Prospero:

> Be cheerful, sir.
> Our revels now are ended. These our actors,
> As I foretold you, were all spirits, and
> Are melted into air, into thin air;
> And like the baseless fabric of this vision,
> The cloud-capped towers, the gorgeous palaces,
> The solemn temples, the great globe itself,
> Yea, all which it inherit, shall dissolve;
> And, like this insubstantial pageant faded,
> Leave not a rack behind. We are such stuff
> As dreams are made on, and our little life
> Is rounded with a sleep.

> (4.1.147–58)

Prospero's reassuring explanation of what's just transpired mutates into a variation on the *theatrum mundi* topos, which morphs again into a prophetic meditation, anchored in the analogy drawn between the theatre and the world, on the end of history, humanity and the planet itself that Prospero foresees.

We're invited to envisage the time, untold ages hence, when 'The cloud-capped towers, the gorgeous palaces, / The solemn temples', the symbols of centuries of 'baseless' institutionalized oppression, will have vanished along with the whole 'insubstantial pageant' in which they have played their shameful parts, ending at last the nightmare of history from which humanity is still striving to awaken. But Shakespeare doesn't leave it at that. Beyond the end of history as we have known it lies the extinction of not only 'the great globe itself', but also 'all which it inherit', the entire species that thought it owned the earth. That Prospero presents this apocalyptic prospect as a reason to 'Be cheerful' appears less bizarre in light of its liberating effect on our perception of whatever time and place we happen to be inhabiting. The sublime conclusion of Prospero's mantic monologue – 'We are such stuff / As dreams are made on, and our little life / Is rounded with a sleep' – adopts the first-person plural he employed at the start ('Our revels now are ended. These our actors …'). It adopts, in other words, a universal human standpoint from which to view the collective destiny of our kind. From this anticipated standpoint at the end of time, the entire history of humanity – 'our little life' – appears as immaterial and ephemeral as our dreams, and its termination in oblivion with the extinction of our species seems as innocuous and welcome as falling asleep at the end of the day.

The effect of Prospero's speech is liberating because, while we listen to it or read it, we step out of the moment in history, the place in the world and the socially conditioned identity to which chance has consigned us, and are transported to a domain beyond time. From there we can look back on everything that has happened, is happening and will happen within time, however terrible or ridiculous it may be, as an 'insubstantial pageant' in which we no longer have a part to play. The speech grants us a fleeting release from mental and emotional thraldom to the selves and lives that bind us by giving us a universal human vantage point from which to view that thraldom. It's the culminating expression of a deep-seated drive to 'jump the life to come' (*Macbeth*, 1.7.7), to flash forward to 'the promised end' (*King Lear*, 5.3.238), that can be discerned throughout Shakespeare's writing. That drive, as we've seen, energizes the poetry that will survive 'Even in the eyes of all posterity / That wear this world out to the ending doom', and it finds a voice in the gravedigger's boast that 'the houses that he makes lasts till doomsday'. But its force can be felt, too, in the speech in which Cressida pledges eternal fidelity to Troilus, and imagines her infidelity, should she prove untrue, being remembered even

When time is old and hath forgot itself,
When water drops have worn the stones of Troy
And blind oblivion swallowed cities up,
And mighty states characterless are grated
To dusty nothing ...

(*Troilus and Cressida*, 3.2.181–5)

And Shakespeare's supreme tragedy, *King Lear*, derives much of its visionary might from dramatizing the inhuman cruelty of Shakespeare's world not just from the standpoint of the utopian era predicted by the Fool ('Then comes the time, who lives to see't / That going shall be used with feet'), but in the certain knowledge that, even if his prediction should one day be fulfilled, the time will also come when 'This great world / Shall so wear out to naught' (4.5.130–1).

IV

The language and the strategies of prophecy are repeatedly conscripted by Shakespeare's poetry and plays to release them from the deterministic grip of the given: to transmute the discourse of historicity into the dialect of possibility, the burden of what has been into a vista of what could be. In an era obsessed with augury and prognostication this oracular cast of mind was far from being peculiar to the man who thought of his books as 'dumb presagers' (Sonnet 23). In his sermon to the king and his court on Christmas Day, 1606, the day before they were entertained by *King Lear*, Lancelot Andrewes reminded his congregation that it's in the nature of prophecy to use the past to address the future, 'speaking of things to come as if they were already past'. If Shakespeare had needed a contemporary philosopher to endorse his doing likewise in his drama, he would have found his favourite philosopher, Montaigne, happy to oblige. In his essay, '*Our affections are transported beyond our selves*', Montaigne rebukes those who 'accuse men for ever gaping after future things' instead of busying themselves with 'present fortunes'. Their admonitions are futile, Montaigne explains, because 'We are never in our selves, but beyond. Feare, desire, and hope, draw us ever towards that which is to come, and remove our sense and consideration from that which is, to amuse us on that which shall be, yea when we shall be no more.'

Kindred spirits professing similar views could be found nearer to home, too, amongst Shakespeare's fellow English poets. '*God* hath imprinted in every *naturall man*,' Donne declares in a sermon, 'an endlesse, and Undeterminable desire of more, then this life can minister unto him' and thus 'leaves man in *expectation*'. For Donne, indeed, the divinely prescribed temporal trajectory of mankind is not only ontologically innate but also the distinguishing feature of our species: 'Creatures of an inferiour nature are possest with the *present*; *Man is a future Creature*.' Spenser plainly felt, like Shakespeare, the pull of futurity on the creative imagination. In his Preface to *The Faerie Queene* he draws a sharp distinction between the method of the 'Historiographer' and the method of the 'Poet historical', who 'thrusteth into the middest, even where it most concerneth him, and there recoursing to the thinges forepaste, and divining of things to come, maketh a pleasing analysis of all'. The idea that Shakespeare's English and Roman history plays, as the work of a dramatic 'Poet historical' could similarly be seen as 'recoursing to the thinges forepaste, and divining of things to come' would have made perfect sense to Spenser. Indeed, the phrase could be stretched to characterize the double dynamic of Shakespearean drama in general: ensconced in the culture and discourse of an age from which it feels exiled, because its spiritual home lies in a future it can foreshadow but not apprehend.

Quotations could be culled from many more early modern English authors to show that the prophetic impetus of Shakespeare's drama found no shortage of parallels among his peers. But the strength and ubiquity of that impetus in his writings were as unparalleled then as they remain today. In previous books, particularly *Shakespeare* and *Shakespeare's Comedies*, as well as in various essays, I've endeavoured to demonstrate its strength and ubiquity in detail. Further corroboration can be found in the surprisingly few modern critics who have also turned their minds to this aspect of Shakespeare's plays. In his pioneering essay 'Past and Future in Shakespeare's Drama', for example, Wolfgang Clemen enlists the history plays, *Hamlet* and *The Tempest* to show how Shakespeare habitually 'weaves retrospect and prognostication into the action as it advances, into the dramatic discourse and conflict'. Joseph Wittreich's equally trailblazing study, *'Image of that Horror': History, Prophecy and Apocalypse in 'King Lear'*, argues compellingly that '*Lear* is an historical mirror in which, beholding the past, we catch prophetic glimpses, however darkly, of the present and future'. No less compelling is Harold Bloom's account of *Macbeth* in *Shakespeare: The Invention of the Human* as a tragedy of the proleptic imagination, a protracted meditation on the dark side of the urge to be 'transported', as Lady Macbeth is by her husband's letter, 'beyond / This ignorant present' in order to 'feel now / The future in the instant'. In 'The Fight for the Future Perfect' in his book *Imaginary Audition*, Harry Berger identifies the future perfect as the master tense of Richard II's imagination, as he commutes between present and future to fashion the past to which death is about to consign him. And in '"What's past is prologue": Temporality and Prophecy in the History Plays', taking her cue from Derrida's discussion of the *futur antérieur* in *Dissemination*, Marjorie Garber demonstrates that 'A similar logic of retrospective anticipation underlies the "prior past that is still to come" in Shakespeare's histories.'

The supreme instance of this 'logic of retrospective anticipation' is the speech delivered in choric couplets to the audience by Time itself at the start of Act 4 of *The Winter's Tale*:

> I that please some, try all; both joy and terror
> Of good and bad; that makes and unfolds error,

Now take upon me in the name of Time
To use my wings. Impute it not a crime
To me or my swift passage that I slide
O'er sixteen years and leave the growth untried
Of that wide gap, since it is in my power
To o'erthrow law, and in one self-born hour
To plant and o'erwhelm custom. Let me pass
The same I am ere ancient'st order was
Or what is now received. I witness to
The times that brought them in; so shall I do
To th' freshest things now reigning, and make stale
The glistering of this present as my tale
Now seems to it. Your patience this allowing,
I turn my glass, and give my scene such growing
As you had slept between.

(4.1.1–17)

With the 'swift passage' of time the 'glistering' present
moment in which we're hearing Time speak these words
right now will pass, and 'th' freshest things now reigning'
– including the sovereign power smuggled in through that
metaphor – will soon seem as stale as the antique tale being
acted on this stage before us. As 'th' argument of Time'
(4.1.29) fast-forwards us to the virtual reality of the future
perfect, what once seemed iron laws are exposed as ephemeral
conventions, while ways of life once regarded as immutable
turn out to have been the creations of 'custom', the transient
dispensations of particular cultures. As surely as the order
of things in 'ancient'st' times strikes the modern world as
obsolete, so 'what is now receiv'd' – what's accepted as
normal not only by Shakespeare's original audience, but also
(the speech implies) by future audiences watching the play
being acted 'In states unborn and accents yet unknown' – is
likewise fated to fade into what used to be.

This extraordinary speech by Time about time articulates
explicitly the vision that implicitly informs, to a greater or
lesser degree, in one way or another, all Shakespeare's plays.

It's a dramatic vision in which the drive to historicize and the drive to prefigure are fused: in which the historical reality of Shakespeare's world is rendered theatrically and poetically from the vantage point of radically different realities already evolving within that world. And insofar as those alternative realities adumbrated by the plays still lie beyond the reach of our time, Shakespeare's dramatizations of his vanished world can empower us to look back upon our world, too, as if we were seeing it through 'eyes not yet created'.

Shakespearean scholars and critics, like literary scholars and critics in general, are professionally prone to study works of literature for the light they shed on the past or on the present. In doing so, they tend to neglect what Fredric Jameson has called 'the utopian projections works of past and present alike offer onto a future otherwise sealed from us'. But to attend to those projections in the works of Shakespeare is not to neglect the obvious respects in which they are entrenched in the world in which they were written. It's rather to engage with the plays on the understanding that they are drawn as strongly towards futures beyond our apprehension as back to their points of origin in early modern England. On this understanding, the key task of a *truly historical* engagement with Shakespeare's plays is to elicit from their language and form what Ernst Bloch calls 'the future in the past that is significant to the degree that the genuine agent of cultural heritage reaches into the past, and in this very same act the past itself anticipates him, involves him and needs him'.

The imperviousness of most academic Shakespeareans to the utopian spell cast by Shakespeare's poetry and plays is especially ironic, given that deciphering portents of the present and the future in the texts of the past clearly wouldn't have struck Shakespeare himself as odd. On the contrary: in Sonnet 106, for example, he expressly adopts the role of a reader discovering the precocious modernity of the poetry of long ago:

When in the chronicle of wasted time

I see descriptions of the fairest wights,
And beauty making beautiful old rhyme
In praise of ladies dead and lovely knights;
Then in the blazon of sweet beauty's best,
Of hand, of foot, of lip, of eye, of brow,
I see their antique pen would have expressed
Even such a beauty as you master now.
So all their praises are but prophecies
Of this our time, all you prefiguring,
And for they looked but with divining eyes
They had not skill enough your worth to sing;

And in *Henry IV Part 2*, in which characters speculate constantly on the relation of the past to the future and the possibility of foreknowledge, Warwick is given this striking speech about tracing the course of the future in the contours of the past:

There is a history in all men's lives,
Figuring the natures of the times deceased;
The which observed, a man may prophesy,
With a near aim, of the main chance of things
As yet not come to life, who in their seeds
And weak beginnings lie intreasurèd.
Such things become the hatch and brood of time;

(3.1.75–81)

In short, we need look no further than Shakespeare himself for a warrant to read his own 'chronicles of wasted time' as 'prophecies / Of this our time' *and* 'of the main chance of things / As yet not come to life', which Shakespeare discerned by looking at life in his time with 'divining eyes', and which he set down with his 'antique pen' for us to interpret afresh in the light of our time.

I believe that the power of Shakespeare's plays to dramatize how things were in his day from the standpoint of how they still could and should be in our day, is the secret source of the quality for which they are tirelessly lauded, and which hard-core historicists have striven in vain to dismiss as a sentimental myth or an ideological delusion: their timelessness. If Coleridge was right about Shakespearean drama being out of step with its time and subsequent times, because it registers the past in a way that projects future possibilities in a wonderful degree, then its manifest capacity to outlive the age in which it was written has nothing to do with reflecting the perennial truths of human experience and everything to do with how far ahead of us its vision of Shakespeare's age remains. That vision is *timeless* precisely because it has yet to be realized and has thus not yet become 'the hatch and brood of time'. And it remains so far ahead of us and 'timeless' in this sense because of its *universality*, by which, as I've already argued and will now try to show in more detail, I mean something quite different from what's usually understood by that concept when it's applied to Shakespeare.

CHAPTER THREE

'This Wide and Universal Theatre'

I

The timeless quality of Shakespeare's drama is indivisible from its universality, because the awareness of the universal human potential to live otherwise that dynamizes his drama dislocates its vision from his time and projects it into the future beyond our time. But the timeless universality of that vision is equally indivisible from his plays' immersion in their moment in history, because it's discovered and articulated in the course of dramatizing, transposed to other times and places, the ineluctable reality of Shakespeare's time and place. The timeless emerges as a dimension of the temporal; the universal is latent in the local and particular; the utopian is secreted within the dystopian facts of history. The universal *potential* of humankind to create a genuinely egalitarian community is not a discarnate abstraction, whose conceptualization precedes the play. It's grasped dramatically and poetically in the process of scripting the play and bringing it to life in the mind or on stage. It crystallizes in the interstices of the actual as a palpable component of the imaginary predicament the play explores. And, precisely because this universal human potential is embedded in the concrete, empirical reality of characters locked in that dramatized predicament, the prospect of its realization acquires a credibility it could not command as an abstract proposition, divorced from the depicted experience of individuals in a version of the world as it is.

A perfect example of what I mean is furnished by Shylock's retort to the Jew-baiting Christians in *The Merchant of Venice*:

> Hath not a Jew eyes? Hath not a Jew hands, organs, dimensions, senses, affections, passions; fed with the same food, hurt with the same weapons, subject to the same diseases, healed by the same means, warmed and cooled by the same winter and summer as a Christian is? If you prick us do we not bleed? If you tickle us do we not laugh? If you poison us do we not die? And if you wrong us shall we not revenge? If we are like you in the rest, we will resemble you in that. If a Jew wrong a Christian, what is his humility? Revenge. If a Christian wrong a Jew, what should his sufferance be by Christian example? Why, revenge. The villainy you teach me I will execute, and it shall go hard but I will better the instruction.
>
> (3.1.54–68)

Shylock rebukes his tormentors on the grounds that they share the same physiology, faculties, emotions and needs, which render them equally vulnerable, equally mortal and equally justified in avenging the wrongs done to them. His arraignment of their anti-Semitism invokes a concept of equality that indicts in effect every form of inhuman discrimination. The irony, of course, is that Shylock is determined to vindicate the compassionate principles to which he appeals by violating them through revenge. But the physically founded concept of equality invoked by Shylock to justify his vengeance eclipses the vindictive purpose for which he enlists it, propelling the vision of the *play*, as distinct from the viewpoint of the *character*, far beyond the Elizabethan age in which it was written, making it as much a play for today as a play for

1596. Shylock is unwittingly enlisted, in other words, as a spokesman for the ethical obligations that arise from our belonging to the same species. As a character whose mind is controlled by his vindictive obsession, Shylock invokes the fact of our generic consanguinity to buttress the rationale of his revenge, not to commend an enlightened precept to the Christians goading him. But Shakespeare puts into Shylock's mouth an argument which has wider egalitarian implications than the Jew is aware of, as the speech's enduring impact attests. The embittered attitude of a demonized revenger, whose heart is trapped in the culture of Shakespeare's day, is brought into tension with the universal perspective, implicit in the potential equality of all human beings, from which that attitude is dramatized. A detailed reading of the whole play as written from this perspective – as deeply committed to the common human cause of 'kindness' (1.3.140–2) that Shylock, Antonio and Portia all betray – can be found in my book *Shakespeare's Comedies*.

Shakespeare places a speech with a similar scope and impact in the mouth of Desdemona's maid, Emilia, in *Othello*. On the cliff-edge of the catastrophe, just before Othello enters to murder Desdemona in the belief that she's cuckolded him with Cassio, mistress and maid fall to talking about the rights and wrongs of committing adultery. After cheerfully confessing that she'd have no compunction about cuckolding her husband if she stood to gain enough by it, Emilia launches into a passionate defence of wives driven to adultery by their husbands' mistreatment of them:

> But I do think it is their husbands' faults
> If wives do fall. Say that they slack their duties,
> And pour our treasures into foreign laps,
> Or else break out in peevish jealousies,
> Throwing restraint upon us; or say they strike us,
> Or scant our former having in despite:
> Why, we have galls; and though we have some grace,
> Yet have we some revenge. Let husbands know

Their wives have sense like them; they see, and smell,
And have their palates both for sweet and sour,
As husbands have. What is it that they do
When they change us for others? Is it sport?
I think it is. And doth affection breed it?
I think it doth. Is't frailty that thus errs?
It is so, too. And have not we affections,
Desires for sport, and frailty, as men have?
Then let them use us well; else let them know,
The ills we do, their ills instruct us so.

(4.3.85–102)

The direct echo of Shylock's speech is unmistakable. Emilia bases her protest at the sexual injustice to which women are subjected by marriage in a patriarchal society on the same irrefutable evidence of physical and emotional affinity that Shylock adduces to upbraid his abusers. The argument she mounts is the cynical response of a worldly-wise wife of her rank conversing informally with her mistress, woman to woman, about the woes of married life in this period. But, once again, while the immediate purpose of the character and the cultural context of the speech remain rooted in their historical moment, the egalitarian rationale of the speech affords *us* a view of the matter – in this case the patriarchal plight of too many women then and now – that points far beyond that moment. That the entire tragedy of *Othello* is charged with the same tension between painful realities and utopian possibilities as Emilia's speech hardly stands in need of demonstration: by falling in love, eloping and marrying, Othello and Desdemona act as if they are free citizens of the fully civilized era whose advent we ourselves await, rather than prisoners of a barbaric epoch, in which racial prejudice and sexual injustice are so deeply ingrained that even their brave hearts are tainted by them.

In both Shylock's speech and Emilia's speech the potential is brought to light by a protest against the injustice of the actual: the innate capacity of human beings to base their attitudes to each other, and their treatment of each other, on what they have in common is discovered through the exposure and indictment of a dehumanizing reality. In neither case does the character advocate the need, or voice a desire, for a dispensation founded on the right of individuals to meet their rightful needs, and fulfil their positive potential, simply by virtue of belonging to the human race. But in both cases the characters' venting of their anger at indefensible forms of discrimination compels them to mount, on incontestable premises, an argument that justifies their threats of retaliation. The fact that the enlightened, egalitarian import of that argument is the last thing on the characters' minds as they speak does not detract from its impact; on the contrary, the impact of the argument is enhanced by its being voiced in response to an actual predicament, which makes it credible and demonstrates its validity.

The same holds true for the extraordinary speech delivered by the King in Act 2 of *All's Well*, where the issue at stake is social rather than racial or sexual inequality. Appalled by the King's commanding him to marry Helen as her reward for curing the monarch of his fatal illness, blue-blooded Bertram refuses point blank to comply because, as he callously puts it: 'She had her breeding at my father's charge. / A poor physician's daughter, my wife? Disdain / Rather corrupt me ever' (2.3.115–17). To which the King, outraged by the arrogant young aristo's brazen insubordination, replies:

> 'Tis only title thou disdain'st in her, the which
> I can build up. Strange is it that our bloods,
> Of colour, weight, and heat, poured all together,
> Would quite confound distinction, yet stands off
> In differences so mighty. If she be
> All that is virtuous, save what thou dislik'st –
> 'A poor physician's daughter' – thou dislik'st
> Of virtue for the name. But do not so.
> From lowest place when virtuous things proceed,
> The place is dignified by th' doer's deed.

Where great additions swell's, and virtue none,
It is a dropsied honour. Good alone
Is good without a name, vileness is so:
The property by what it is should go,
Not by the title.

(2.3.118–32)

The King's immediate aim in this speech, which runs on for another 14 lines, is to bend Bertram to his will by the force of argument before resorting, as he subsequently does, to the threat of force. But his reasoning rests, like Shylock's and Emilia's, on the fundamental physiological identity of all human creatures, once the 'additions', the cultural trappings of their place and time, have been stripped away. The basic biological fact that the same red blood, whose physical qualities are identical, flows through the veins of everyone, including the King himself ('*our* bloods'), makes nonsense of the notion that the nobility are a breed apart, kicking away one of the principal props of the King's own sovereignty. Indeed, it can be said to 'confound distinction' altogether, for it shows that the 'differences so mighty', whether of rank or any other kind, that are so deeply entrenched in society have no basis in biology. On the contrary: our literal consanguinity as human beings provides the basis for a society in which the shared needs and interests of its members take precedence over the contrived disparities that set them at odds with each other.

The King, needless to say, draws no such conclusion from the homogeneity implicit in our collective dependence on the same vital fluid. Even he, however, is struck by the 'strange', illogical state of affairs over which he presides as the royal mainstay of 'mighty differences'. And he proceeds to contend, in the same surprisingly enlightened vein, that the true measure of an individual's nobility is their character and conduct, not their rank and title, which he dismisses as worthless attributes in themselves. That contention triggers in turn a scalding denunciation of those who make a fetish of the 'honour' they derive from their ancestors, from the accident of their birth instead of from their deeds:

> The mere word's a slave,
> Debauched on every tomb, on every grave
> A lying trophy, and as oft is dumb
> Where dust and damned oblivion is the tomb
> Of honoured bones indeed.
>
> (2.3.138–42)

The echo of Falstaff's caustic demystification of honour as 'a mere scutcheon' (*1 Henry IV*, 5.1.140) is unmissable. What's so startling is that it should come from the mouth of a monarch, who denounces the titled dead without exception ('on *every* tomb, on *every* grave') as defilers of the honour to which their grand, escutcheoned tombs lay claim, and who regards the unmarked graves of the nameless dead as the more likely repositories of human remains that deserve to be honoured.

It's perhaps no more startling, however, than hearing a monarch base his case on the universal truth that blood flows through the body of every living human being, since he thereby aligns himself with the vilified Jew who asks, 'If you prick us do we not bleed?' and the Prince of Morocco in the same play, of whose failure at the casket test Portia tartly remarks 'Let all of his complexion choose me so' (2.7.79), unmoved by the Moor's magnificent speech upon arriving in Belmont:

> Mislike me not for my complexion,
> The shadowed livery of the burnished sun,
> To whom I am a neighbour and near bred.
> Bring me the fairest creature northward born,
> Where Phoebus' fire scarce thaws the icicles,
> And let us make incision for your love
> To probe whose blood is reddest, his or mine.
>
> (*The Merchant of Venice*, 2.1.1–7)

Oblivious to the alliance with such disparaged aliens his speech has forged, the King concludes it by assuring Bertram that, if he can persuade himself to like 'this creature' Helen 'as a maid', then he, the King, 'can create the rest. Virtue and she / Is her own dower; honour and wealth from me' (2.2.143–5). Equally oblivious to the inconsistency of this proposal with his avowed contempt for the 'dropsied honour' artificially acquired with a title, the King offers to manufacture the nobility that the 'poor physician's daughter' lacks. He offers to endow her, in other words, with the extraneous attributes of the 'distinction' that the classless human bond of blood confounds.

I'm not suggesting for a moment that the King in *All's Well* should be taken as a closet Leveller *avant la lettre*. The King's objective at this point is to bring Bertram to heel by first inducing and finally forcing him to marry Helen, whether either of them likes it or not. 'My honour's at the stake,' he declares, when inducement fails; 'which to defeat / I must produce my power' (2.3.150–1). His overriding priority is not to undermine but to secure his rigidly hierarchical regime, even if it means fabricating by royal fiat the nobility that ought to be hereditary. But the speech Shakespeare writes for him resorts to a line of reasoning that contradicts the logic on which that regime depends, exposing a faultline in the foundations of the status quo. It reveals an egalitarian train of thought emerging and gaining traction within a fictitious early modern mind, in spite of its absolute commitment to institutionalized inequality. The egalitarian attitude engendered by what human beings have in common is caught as it springs inexorably from the conflict between humanity and hierarchy provoked by the plot. And the prospect of a society in which that attitude prevails, far from being crushed by the weight of the status quo, gains strength and empirical authority from being born of that conflict.

The plausibility of the prospect is buttressed, too, by the levelling logic of the play as a whole, to which the King's speech provides the key; for what else does *All's Well* boil down to but a social and sexual revenge comedy, in which the epitome of patrician misogyny gets his comeuppance from 'a poor physician's daughter', in a play penned by a glover's boy from the sticks, who knew, as the *Sonnets* attest, the pain of loving 'a bright particular star' (1.1.85) out of his orbit? The King himself, moreover – or rather, the actor who has been playing the King – distils the spirit of the comedy in the first line of the Epilogue, whose punning plea for applause collapses the arbitrary 'differences so mighty' around which the plot has revolved: 'The King's a beggar now the play is done.'

In fact, that line can be seen as encapsulating the spirit of Shakespearean drama as a whole. For it compresses into a single resonant sentence the conflict that is the driving force of Shakespeare's dramatic vision: the creative conflict between the unconditioned human potential incarnate in the actor and the hierarchy of socially prescribed roles, from king to beggar, to which that potential is reduced once the actor is cast and the performance begins. The retrospective angle outside the play from which the line is delivered is a crucial aspect of its effect. As the actor sheds his regal role, 'now the play is done', he invites the audience, addressing them directly, to look back on this stage-play world of kings and beggars, which they inhabit too, from a point beyond it. Nor can the playfulness of this line, which closes the gulf between monarch and mendicant, conceal its insinuation that reducing a king to a beggar, figuratively speaking, and dissolving the difference between them, was precisely what the play meant to do by the time it was done.

II

These three speeches, by Shylock, Emilia and the King in *All's Well*, should go some way towards illustrating what I mean by the *utopian realism* of Shakespeare's drama, and what Marcuse had in mind when he wrote what I quoted in Chapter 1: 'The utopia in great art is never the simple negation of the reality principle but its transcending preservation [*Aufhebung*] in which past and present cast their shadow on fulfilment.' Because Shakespeare's plays dramatize the historical reality of their time in such three-dimensional depth and solid, sensuous detail, the universalizing perspective from which they dramatize it is charged with a power, and a capacity to convince, that it would not otherwise possess. 'Even the process of wish-fulfilment', as Fredric Jameson observes in *Archaeologies of the Future*, 'includes a kind of reality principle of its own, intent on not making things too easy for itself, accumulating the objections and the reality problems that stand in its way so as the more triumphantly and "realistically" to overcome them'. The three speeches I've cited demonstrate vividly, in short, the sense in which the dramatic art of Shakespeare, to quote Marcuse again, 'has recognized what is and what could be, within and beyond social conditions'.

The plays' recognition of what could and should be is rooted, as the speeches just quoted make clear, in their pervasive alertness to every irrefutable fact that 'makes the whole world kin' (*Troilus and Cressida*, 3.3.169) and provides a standpoint from which to view and judge everything that prevents the universal kinship of which humanity is capable from becoming a reality. That egalitarian awareness didn't spring up from nowhere, of course. Nor was Shakespeare alone in acquiring access to it. As Marx explains in the *Grundrisse*, the levelling dynamic of the early modern market economy engendered a new dimension of experience and consciousness. The system of exchange-value is defined by Marx as 'a system of general social metabolism, of *universal* social relations, of all-round needs and *universal* capacities' (my italics). On the foundations of this system there begins to rise a consciousness of the common human needs and capacities transecting actual economic, social, racial and sexual divisions, which can now be recognized as socially constructed rather than divinely ordained or natural.

As Agnes Heller explains in her classic study *Renaissance Man*, the early modern epoch heralds nothing less than the materialist discovery of the human species, the forging of a radically new conception of 'humanity'. It's the discovery that, in Donne's celebrated formulation, 'No Man is an *Iland*, intire of it selfe; every man is a peece of the *Continent*, a part of the *maine* ... Any Mans *death* diminishes *me*, because I am involved in *Mankinde*'; or, as Montaigne puts it, 'chaque homme porte la forme entière de l'humaine condition', which Florio renders as 'Every man beareth the whole stampe of humane condition'. Nor does Montaigne ascribe this attribute to the male gender alone, since 'les masles et femelles sont jettez en mesme moule; sauf l'institution et l'usage, la différence n'y est pas grande'; or as Florio puts it: 'both male and female, are cast in one same moulde; instruction and custom excepted, there is no great difference between them'. Such statements entail the understanding that each individual, whatever their rank, gender, race, creed or nationality, is *at the same time* a human being, whose equality with the rest of their kind by virtue of that fact entitles them to be treated, and obliges them to treat others, in a manner consistent with their belonging to the same species.

In Donne, moreover, one finds the same visionary leap as one finds in Shakespeare, from the fact of our common humanity to the utopian desire for an egalitarian community. 'All mankind is of one Author, and is one volume', Donne writes in his *Devotions upon Emergent Occasions*; 'when one Man dies, one Chapter is not torn out of the booke, but translated into a better language; and every Chapter must be so translated'. What Donne means by mankind's translation into a better language, from which no one must be excluded, is made plain in his description of heaven in the *Sermons* as a place 'where there shall be no Cloud nor Sun, no darknesse nor dazzling but one equall light, no noyse nor silence but one equall musick, no fears nor hopes but one equall possession, no foes nor friends but one equall communion and Identity, no ends nor beginnings but one equall eternity'. Here, couched in metaphysical Christian terms, we have Donne's discursive religious version of the secular humanist vision that informs Shakespeare's plays, including their anticipation of a timeless state of universal human equality beyond the inhuman time of history, a state of transfigured consciousness for Donne, in which there shall be 'no ends nor beginnings but one equall eternity'.

For Shakespeare, though, 'the prophetic soul / Of the wide world' is 'dreaming on things to come' in this world not the next, however long the wide world is destined to wait. Shakespeare may share with Donne, Montaigne and any number of his more enlightened contemporaries the awareness that he, like every other person on earth, is 'involved in *Mankinde*' and thus 'beareth the whole stampe of humane condition'. But what sets him apart from them is the fact that his drama is not only *structured and directed* by this awareness, but also sympathetically alive to its subversive political implications and intent on making them dramatically and poetically explicit. In Robert Winder's novel *The Final Act of Mr Shakespeare*, Edward Alleyn explains to John Donne's daughter that Shakespeare 'marches to a different tune' and is 'not quite like the rest of us', because his drama is driven by one overriding idea: 'Shakespeare's idea is simply this: that worms will gnaw on kings and knaves alike. It is so simple that it is easy to forget it. Shakespeare's strength is that he *never* forgets it.' To which it's tempting to add that the weakness of most Shakespearean criticism to date is that it has found Shakespeare's simple idea all too easy to forget, and thus remained blind to the revolutionary ramifications of his egalitarian vision.

For those whose purely retrospective view of history, and of Shakespeare's place in it, baulks at the characterization of his dramatic vision as egalitarian, let alone revolutionary, it's worth recalling the points made about *Hamlet* in the previous chapter and putting the broad political thrust of the play beyond doubt. Terminally alienated from everything his rank entails, including the obligation to revenge his royal father's murder, the disaffected prince vents his contempt for what the disabused Lear derides as 'the great image of authority' (4.5.154). 'The King is a thing ... Of nothing' (4.2.27–9), Hamlet retorts to Rosencrantz, but it soon becomes clear that it's not merely Claudius but monarchy, and indeed hierarchy itself, that he has in mind, when he proceeds to show Claudius 'how a king may go a progress through the guts of a beggar' – 'Your fat king and your lean beggar' being 'two dishes, but to one table', since the corpses of both wind up as food for maggots. The play's levelling vision emerges fully in the graveyard scene in the banter of the gravedigger as he labours with his spade and the prince's ensuing exchange with this wise fool on an equal verbal footing, which abolishes the normally insuperable barrier between them. In this audacious scene Hamlet's tragic, class-bound plight as the son of a king, stranded in that society at that moment in history, is placed in a classless, transhistorical perspective: a perspective which reaches back, via the gravedigger's canny quips, to our common human origin in Adam before class society (5.1.29–37) and forward to Doomsday, when all the breathers of this world, irrespective of their rank, riches or power when alive, will be granted equal rights in the ultimate democracy of death.

'[A]nd now my Lady Worm's, chapless, and knocked about the mazard with a sexton's spade', muses Hamlet, as he contemplates one of the skulls tossed up by the gravedigger. 'Here's fine revolution, an we had the trick to see't' (5.1.86–9). The strict historicist scholar will hasten to point out that the word 'revolution' must be construed here as a reference to the wheel of fortune or the whirligig of time, and that to impute our modern political meaning to it would be anachronistic. It would indeed, but it would also be perfectly in keeping with Shakespeare's profoundly anachronistic imagination. Given the dramatic context in which Hamlet uses the word, it would be perverse not to perceive its modern political meaning already breaking through here, especially when it can also be seen surfacing in Henry IV's wish 'that one might read the book of fate, / And see the revolution of the times / Make mountains level' (3.1.44–6). As George Steiner observes in *After Babel*: 'Shakespeare at times seems to "hear" inside a word or phrase the history of its future echoes.'

The broader point here bears repeating in order to counter predictable objections. It's obviously not that Shakespeare was alone in perceiving that death lays its icy hands on kings and commoners alike, reminding us that what binds human beings together is more powerful and enduring than the cultural fictions that divide them, which are shadows, not substantial things by comparison. It's not just that Shakespeare never let go of this widespread perception either, vital though it is to keep this fact in mind while reading and watching his plays. It's rather that Shakespeare understood the subversive significance of the fact that 'every man is a peece of the *Continent*, a part of the *maine*' and developed this understanding into a comprehensive dramatic vision beyond anything his fellow dramatists were capable of conceiving. The comprehensive nature of that vision needs stressing, because its articulation is not confined to the overt egalitarian insights and attitudes voiced with such arresting eloquence in speeches and exchanges like the ones I've been quoting.

The gravedigger's riddling repartee about Adam being the first true gentleman, because he was the first to bear arms – the arms he used to dig with, just like the gravedigger as he speaks – echoes the text on which John Ball famously preached during the Peasants' Revolt of 1381: 'When Adam delved and Eve span, / Who was then the gentleman?' And of what he fancies might well be the skull of a gentleman, in this case a lawyer, Hamlet wryly remarks: 'Why does he suffer this rude knave now to knock him about the sconce with a dirty shovel, and will not tell him of his action of battery?' (5.1.97–100). But no less powerful, indeed arguably more powerful, than the levelling tenor of both characters' speeches is the breathtaking boldness of bringing a disaffected intellectual prince and this shrewdly irreverent, nameless labourer into free, unconstrained conversation with each other on stage as the latter actually works. It's an encounter and an exchange that may be without precedence in theatrical history, although not without parallels in Shakespeare's own oeuvre. That Shakespeare could stage such a scene at such a crucial point in the tragedy, and allow the wise plebeian fool, the only character in the play to share Hamlet's antic language of licensed equivocation, to quibble the prince into submission, speaks volumes in itself about the standpoint from which he wrote. It's a standpoint that's not only expressed in the form of statements made in speeches, but that's dramatically embodied and visibly enacted – that's *performed* on the stage – as well.

The full measure of an exchange like the bout of badinage between the gravedigger and Hamlet can be taken only by taking into account the terms on which, as well as the terms in which, the dialogue is conducted and staged. For only then does the key question begged by such exchanges become apparent: from what position, and on what understanding, must the dramatist be writing in order to find such a dialogue not just conceivable but desirable and indispensable at that vital juncture in the play? Or, to put the question another way: what assumptions, values and ideals does the creation of such a groundbreaking scene between such incongruous characters presuppose on the part of the playwright who penned it?

III

The basic idea of the graveyard scene is, after all, not only far from unparalleled in the rest of Shakespeare's plays, but a hallmark of his habitual mode of composition. For corroboration of this claim in a different genre one need only turn to *Henry V*. 'I think the King is but a man, as I am', says the disguised Henry to the foot soldier Bates on the eve of Agincourt. 'The violet smells to him as it doth to me; the element shows to him as it doth to me. All his senses have but human conditions. His ceremonies laid by, in his nakedness he appears but a man' (4.1.101–5). Here Shakespeare uses the plural of the same term Florio employs in his version of Montaigne's declaration that 'Every man beareth the whole stampe of humane condition' – the word 'human' being likewise spelled 'humane' in the First Folio text of Henry's speech, as it is throughout the First Folio. But note how, in marked contrast to the lucubrations of Montaigne and the religious homilies and meditations of Donne, Shakespeare exploits the seditious implications of the human dimension to undermine hierarchy and rob sovereignty of its absolute authority. He does this by contriving an extraordinary imaginary confrontation between ruler and ruled, through which these seditious implications become apparent, without obscuring in the slightest the obdurate reality of the sovereign's supremacy in the world beyond the Globe. Henry's royalty is cushioned, of course, against the demystifying impact of his speech to Bates by the advantage his disguise confers on him and the ironic humour it invites the audience to enjoy at the common soldiers' expense. But that doesn't save the King of England from being put in the dock on the public stage by those soldiers and forced to justify the cynically concocted war in which they are about to risk their lives.

No other dramatist of the day had the nerve or the skill to devise with impunity a scene which allows one common soldier to say of his monarch to his monarch on the eve of battle: 'I would he were here alone. So should he be sure to be ransomed, and a many poor men's lives saved' (4.1.120–2); and which compels his royal highness to improvise an unconvincing response to this devastating charge levelled by another:

> But if the cause be not good, the King himself hath a heavy reckoning to make, when all those legs and arms and heads chopped off in a battle shall join together at the latter day, and cry all, 'We died at such a place' – some swearing, some crying for a surgeon, some upon their wives left poor behind them, some upon the debts they owe, some upon their children rawly left. I am afeard there are few die well

that die in a battle, for how can they charitably dispose of anything, when blood is their argument? Now, if these men do not die well, it will be a black matter for the King that led them to it – who to disobey were against all proportion of subjection.

(4.1.133–45)

That this charge hits home and Henry takes it to heart is clear from the soliloquy he delivers after the soldiers leave, in which he bemoans the 'hard condition, / Twin-born with greatness' that he must endure as the price of his throne: 'What infinite heartsease / Must kings neglect that private men enjoy?' (4.1.230–1, 233–4). But this stock trope, which frames the whole soliloquy, is sabotaged by the blinding realization from which the routine sentiment of the speech never recovers. When it comes right down to it, Henry must confess, the only thing that separates king from commoner, constraining the latter to kneel in 'adoration', in 'awe and fear', to the former, and be sent to his death by him if so ordered, is the 'idol ceremony' (4.1.237, 242, 244). And the essence of the 'thrice-gorgeous ceremony' with which sovereigns secure the abject 'adulation', the perpetual 'flexure and low bending' of their subjects? Nothing but 'place, degree, and form' (4.1.243, 251–2, 263), whose capacity to mystify and enthrall derives from no power inherent in the object of adulation, but is conjured up by a dazzling display of regal paraphernalia:

> the balm, the sceptre, and the ball,
> The sword, the mace, the crown imperial,
> The intertissued robe of gold and pearl,
> The farcèd title running fore the king,
> The throne he sits on ...

(4.1.257–61)

To be sure, Henry piles up the imposing regalia of majesty in order to weigh all that they signify against the good fortune of 'the wretched slave / Who with a body filled and vacant mind /

Gets him to rest, crammed with distressful bread', unlike the care-worn king, forced to lie awake throughout the 'horrid night, the child of hell' (4.1.265–7). He marshals them, in other words, in the service of an age-old argument designed to defend sovereigns against their detractors by assuring them that those born to rule them are to be pitied rather than envied. But by the time Henry reaches the punchline of this protracted apologia, which was prompted by his exchange with Bates and Williams, it's too late. It's too late, that is, to retract his acknowledgement that the only difference between him and the likes of them, besides an accident of birth, is a glamorous costume, glittering arcane props and an interminable string of grandiose titles. (Henry's disdain for the latter is succinctly conveyed by the line 'The farcèd title running fore the king', which personifies the barrage of honorifics that precedes the monarch's entrance as a fat, overfed courtier ushering him in.)

In this regard the soliloquy echoes and reinforces the egalitarian impetus of Henry's remark to Bates when they first meet: 'I think the King is but a man, as I am … His ceremonies laid by, in his nakedness he appears but a man'. It does so, however, without cancelling Henry's conscription of the soliloquy to shore up the very institution that his own reasoning, and his exposure to incrimination by Bates and Williams, have undermined. But to construe the soliloquy, or the scene as a whole, on that ground as an admirable example of Shakespeare's supposed 'impartiality' is to be guilty of evasive complacency. Shakespeare is not giving the king and the commoners an equal say in an even-handed debate without coming down on either side. What Shakespeare does in this scene, first and foremost, is exploit the theatrical licence of disguise to stage an otherwise unthinkable encounter and exchange, the mere fact of whose staging is a clear index of the dramatist's standpoint. This licensed exchange allows common soldiers to say on the public stage what they really think about their king to his face, and the king to come clean to himself and the audience, through the fictive intimacy of soliloquy, about the fact that his sovereignty is a culturally contrived illusion.

None of this changes a thing about the situation, let alone the world and time, in which the characters find themselves. At no point in the scene is the inescapable reality of a social order ruled by kings, who have absolute power over their subjects, denied or a more equitable alternative to it envisaged, demanded or prescribed. On the contrary: that inescapable reality is fully registered by being vividly embodied in richly characterized figures, voicing their thoughts in terms which are tailored to their rank, their imagined personalities, and the views such characters might well hold at such a time in such a place, in order to render them believable. But the lens through which the scene is dramatized and worded is bifocal: we behold the immediate, intransigent actuality of the social order that still prevailed in Shakespeare's day, but within the wider, longer perspective produced by the disclosure of unrealized human potentiality pressing against the irrational constraints of that order.

The creative tension between actual and potential that generates the bifocal vision not just of this scene, but of *Henry V* as a whole and of all Shakespeare's plays, is encapsulated in the disguised Henry's equivocal statement, 'I think the King is but a man, as I am', whose humour depends on the audience's complicity. For the statement keeps in focus both Henry's ineradicable royal identity and destiny, to which the audience alone is privy at this moment, and the equally ineradicable fact that 'All his senses have but human conditions', leaving nothing to distinguish him from the 'base, common, and popular' (4.1.39) but mere 'ceremony', as he subsequently admits to himself. The statement does not warrant the half-baked inference, on the part of audience or reader, that deep down we're all the same, so the fact that Henry happens to be a king and his soldiers happen to be 'base, common, and popular' doesn't fundamentally matter. Henry's royalty, and the whole inequitable order of things it implies, are not erased by his saying that he is 'but a man' subject to the same 'human conditions' as everyone else. On the contrary, their indelible reality is insisted on, sharpening the contradiction between all that human beings are capable of becoming, simply by virtue of being human, and their confinement in the oppressive roles imposed on them by the divisive society they have the misfortune to inhabit.

IV

I've dwelt on this sentence, and on the scene in which it proves so pivotal, partly because they show so clearly how Shakespeare's simultaneous grasp of historical realities and utopian possibilities finds expression in his diction, in the fine grain of his phrasing, as well as in the dialogic design and composition of a whole scene. But I've dwelt on them mainly because, once the points they seek to illustrate are granted, their bearing on the entire range of his dramatic output becomes much plainer.

They have an obvious direct bearing, for example, on our understanding of Lear's storm-lashed encounter with Edgar in the guise of the mad Bedlam beggar, Poor Tom. No sooner has a mortified Lear envisaged the 'Poor naked wretches' he has neglected, whose 'houseless heads and unfed sides' must 'bide the pelting of this pitiless storm' (3.4.28–30), than a real poor naked wretch materializes before him. 'Thou wert better in a grave', says the homeless king to the houseless beggar, 'than to answer with thy uncovered body this extremity of the skies':

> Is man no more than this? Consider him well. Thou owest the worm no silk, the beast no hide, the sheep no wool, the cat no perfume. Ha, here's three on's are sophisticated; thou art the thing itself. Unaccommodated man is no more but such a poor, bare, forked animal as thou art. Off, off, you lendings! Come, unbutton here.
>
> (3.4.95–103)

It's an astounding moment, rendered all the more astounding by the fact that *King Lear* 'was played at Whitehall before the

King's Majesty upon St Stephen's night in Christmas holidays', as the title page of the 1608 quarto informs us. Before the audience's eyes King James's legendary, omnipotent precursor on the throne of Albion is robbed of his sovereignty, his sanity and the roof over his head, and forced by 'The tyranny of the open night', which is 'too rough / For nature to endure' (3.4.2–3), to feel for the first time what the poor naked wretches of his kingdom feel: hunger, cold and despair.

Undaunted, however, by his audacity in dreaming up such a scenario and laying himself open to the charge of *lèse-majesté*, Shakespeare refuses to leave it at that. He invents an encounter that compels the king to realize that beneath his royal robes and a mad beggar's rags shivers the same 'poor, bare, forked animal', the same 'Unaccommodated man', and to *enact* that realization on stage by tearing off his robes, the tawdry trappings of majesty that Lear now derides as mere 'lendings', because he knows he has no innate right to possess them. Lear's confrontation with Poor Tom brings home with harrowing force the full import of Henry's statement, 'I think the King is but a man, as I am ... His ceremonies laid by, in his nakedness he appears but a man', precisely by acting it out and making it dramatically *visible*. It also acts out the subversive insight secreted in the opening line of the Epilogue of *All's Well*: 'The King's a beggar now the play is done.' For once the curtain has fallen on the absurd autocratic farce in which Lear played the lead for so long, the human identity he shares with the beggar before him becomes not just undeniable but physically demonstrable, as Lear attempts to prove.

The fact that Edgar is actually a nobleman impersonating a demented beggar detracts not a whit from the scene's impact and significance. On the contrary, it reinforces them. By having Edgar adopt Poor Tom as his alter ego, Shakespeare reveals the 'poor, bare, forked animal' normally concealed by the costly 'lendings' adorning the aristocracy to distinguish them at a glance from their ill-clad inferiors. The shattering truth Lear discovers and articulates as he addresses Poor Tom is already graphically incarnate, before Lear opens his mouth, in the helpless human creature facing him, whose body is at once a lord's and a beggar's, as well as the body of the actor who fuses them together by playing them both.

The whole tragedy of *King Lear* turns on the conflict between Lear's hierarchically determined fate and the unconditioned human potential which that fate violates: between a demented monarch bound upon a wheel of fire and 'the thing itself', the 'unaccommodated man' that survives as pure potentiality within everyone, everywhere, in every age, and thus is capable of binding us all together, past, present and future, as one species, in defiance of everything that divides us. Through the traumatic transformations of Lear, Gloucester and Edgar the play demolishes the pillars of disparity that support all forms of class society, and the unequal distribution of wealth and power on which class society depends. It climaxes in a regal snarl of contempt for all who arrogate to themselves the right to impose their will on others: 'A dog's obeyed in office' (4.5.154–5). And in place of institutionalized greed, exploitation and oppression the tragedy advocates a compassionate egalitarian ethic founded on the kinship of all human creatures: 'So distribution should undo excess, / And each man have enough' (4.1.64–5).

At such moments the moral and political corollaries of the universalizing imagination that covertly governs the plays find overt expression. Such moments may be rare, but they are no less noteworthy for that. The conclusion to which bitter experience drives the blind Earl of Gloucester requires that punitive retribution be visited upon 'the superfluous and lust-dieted man' – men, that is, just like his former self – who 'will not see / Because he does not feel', in order that the wealth of society can be shared out equally between everyone. It's a conclusion that links the disabused Earl, in an otherwise unlikely political alliance, with the rebel Jack Cade, whose battle-cries are 'All the realm shall be in common' (4.2.70) and 'henceforward all things shall be in common' (4.7.17); with the Gardener in *Richard II*, who pointedly instructs his workmate in the hearing of the Queen: 'Go thou, and,

like an executioner, / Cut off the heads of too fast-growing
sprays / That look too lofty in our commonwealth. / All must
be even in our government' (3.4.34–7); with the gravedigger
in *Hamlet*, who regards it as 'the more pity that great folk
should have count'nance in this world to drown or hang
themselves more than their even Christian', which prompts
the reflection, as he continues to dig ('Come my spade') that
'There is no ancient gentlemen but gardeners, ditchers and
gravemakers; they hold up Adam's profession' (5.1.26–31);
and with the fisherman overheard by the shipwrecked prince
Pericles explaining to his mates, as they labour with their nets,
that fish live in the sea 'as men do a-land – the great ones eat
up the little ones. I can compare our rich misers to nothing so
fitly as to a whale: a plays and tumbles, driving the poor fry
before him, and at last devours them all at a mouthful. Such
whales have I heard on o'th' land, who never leave gaping till
they swallowed the whole parish.' Nor does the fisherman
leave us in any doubt about the solution to this problem. 'We
would purge the land', he declares, 'of these drones that rob
the bee of her honey' (Scene 5, 69–75, 87–8).

The really radical thing about such speeches, however,
is not so much what the speakers say as the proof they
provide of Shakespeare's bent for devising scenes calculated to
generate such speeches or, more commonly, to imply through
dialogue or immediate juxtaposition a class-transcending
standpoint consistent with such speeches. It's Shakespeare's
capacity to conceive and construct not just scenes, but whole
plays in these terms that sets the plays apart, because it's the
capacity to perceive things theatrically and poetically from the
virtual viewpoint of humanity as a whole rather than from
the viewpoint of a particular section of society as it stood in
Shakespeare's day.

That's how we're being invited to perceive things when, at
the tragic climax of *Antony and Cleopatra*, Shakespeare has
an obvious kissing cousin of the gravedigger, in the shape of
a nameless fellow 'Clowne' (as both are called in the First
Folio), force his way into the Egyptian queen's death scene to

quibble with her in the anachronistic idiom of an Elizabethan yokel and bring her 'liberty' (5.2.233) coiled in a basket of figs. The clown's democratic right to share the stage with the queen, and even steal the spotlight from her, is dramatically asserted through a dialogue which *performs* the rhetorical erasure of rank that recurs throughout the denouement, and that is so movingly expressed in Cleopatra's response to Iras's anguished cry, 'Royal Egypt, Empress!': 'No more but e'en a woman, and commanded / By such poor passion as the maid that milks / And does the meanest chores' (4.16.74–7).

A similar effect is achieved in *Macbeth* by the jocular intrusion of the Porter in the immediate aftermath of Duncan's murder, when the knocking at the gate begins. This wry plebeian menial's self-portrait as the 'porter of hell-gate', who 'had thought to have let in some of all professions that go the primrose way to th'everlasting bonfire' (2.3.1–2, 17–18), switches us into a sharply contrasting view of his homicidal master's plight. The three damned souls he imagines knocking at the gate are all encrypted avatars of Macbeth – 'a farmer that hanged himself on th'expectation of plenty', 'an equivo-cator ... who committed treason enough for God's sake, yet could not equivocate to heaven', and 'an English tailor come hither for stealing' (2.3.4–5, 8–11, 12–13). The riddling patter of this wise fool masquerading as a 'devil-porter' provides a ribald prose burlesque of the self-destructive bind in which Macbeth's manhood is at stake: 'much drink may be said to be an equivocator with lechery: it makes him and it mars him' (2.3.16, 30–1). By restating 'the imperial theme' (1.3.128) at this climactic juncture in an irreverent, demotic key, Shakespeare simultaneously underscores and effaces every-thing that divides the regicidal nobleman from the crapulent lackey cracking lewd gags at his expense.

The visible and audible social disparity between the Porter and Macbeth is underscored by placing them cheek by jowl at the same dreadful moment; but by placing them cheek by jowl at the same dreadful moment, and having the Porter regale the audience with a vulgar comic version of Macbeth's tragic plight, the playwright also constructs for the audience a viewpoint wider than that of either character: a virtual viewpoint that collapses hierarchy by cutting Macbeth down to size. Like the incongruous coupling of Hamlet with the gravedigger, King Lear with Poor Tom, Henry V with Bates and Williams, or Cleopatra with the clown, the structural conjunction of the Porter and Macbeth is a perfect example of Shakespeare's multivocal method of composition in action. It illustrates perfectly the fact that Shakespeare's creation of a universal human perspective on the world as he knew it is as much a matter of form as a matter of phrasing, a question of structure as well as a question of style.

'Form serves as a necessary bridge to new, still unknown content', observes Mikhail Bakhtin: a bridge that leads in Shakespeare's case to what remains for us a 'new, still unknown' future. And, as Theodor Adorno explains, in order to view the past or the present from the virtual standpoint of that utopian future, 'Perspectives must be fashioned that displace and estrange the world, reveal it to be, with its rifts and crevices, as indigent and distorted as it will appear one day in the messianic light.' In the Porter scene, as in all the scenes and speeches I've cited in this chapter, we can see these perspectives, these strategies of displacement and estrangement, being fashioned by a consummate fusion of formal design and poetic diction. Let me recall what I quoted from Marcuse in Chapter 1: 'Inasmuch as man and nature are constituted by an unfree society, their repressed and distorted potentialities can be represented only in an *estranging* form.' The scenes and speeches I've cited in this chapter reveal Shakespeare forging 'the estranging language and images' that make the 'repressed and distorted potentialities' of human beings as 'perceptible, visible and audible' as the human cost of that repression and distortion. It's the capacity to make perceptible by these means the potential possessed by human beings to emancipate themselves that endows Shakespeare's dramatic art with its universal quality.

V

Not the least disconcerting aspect of *Macbeth* is Shakespeare's revelation of that emancipatory potential in a blood-stained regicide, whose henchmen brutally murder a child on stage before his mother's and the audience's eyes. It's first revealed by Lady Macbeth in a phrase that's passed into common parlance as a cliché and lost all its original potency as a result: 'Yet do I fear thy nature', she reflects in her husband's absence, 'It is too full o'th' milk of human kindness / To catch the nearest way' (1.5.15–16). The diction and the imagery Shakespeare employs in the famous phrase require close scrutiny to restore their full effect. The word 'human', as I've already mentioned, is spelled 'humane' in the First Folio. In Shakespeare's day the term 'humane' had not yet split into two separate words with cognate but distinct meanings. So in its original form in Lady Macbeth's line it conflates the descriptive term 'human', meaning characteristic of the genus *homo*, and the prescriptive term 'humane', meaning compassionate. The implication that being human and being humane are inseparable is reinforced by the noun that the adjective 'human/humane' qualifies. 'Kindness' is fully charged here with its early modern import: it means sympathetic, benevolent conduct consistent with one's belonging to the same *kind* as the person to whom kindness is shown. By his own wife's reluctant admission, the future homicide Macbeth is 'too full' of all the qualities condensed in these two words.

No less remarkable is the fact that Macbeth's 'human[e] kindness' is metaphorically described as 'milk'. For this links the phrase subliminally with the nourishing milk the infant sucks from its mother's breast, as Lady Macbeth confirms 30 lines later, when she prays to the forces of evil to be unsexed and filled 'from the crown to the toe top-full / Of direst cruelty': 'Come to my woman's breasts,' she pleads, 'And take my milk for gall, you murd'ring ministers' (1.5.40–2, 46–7). Two short scenes later, in her electrifying argument with

Macbeth, she seizes on the same imagery as she strives to steel his nerves for murder:

> I have given suck, and know
> How tender 'tis to love the babe that milks me.
> I would, while it was smiling in my face,
> Have plucked my nipple from his boneless gums
> And dashed the brains out, had I so sworn
> As you have done to this.
>
> (1.7.54–9)

Here the image of a breastfeeding baby implicit in the image of a mother's milk becomes graphically explicit.

The reason why Shakespeare's evocation of helpless human infancy matters so much is made plain in the stunning soliloquy with which Macbeth opens the play's seventh scene. The speech displays the same tension as Shylock's speech rebuking his tormentors: the tension between the historically defined mind of an individual shaped by a particular culture and a universal human perspective that reaches back through history from the transformed future it foreshadows. Macbeth's fear that Duncan's assassination will incur retribution in 'the life to come' gives way to a review of the grounds for also fearing 'judgement here' (1.7.7–8): to murder Duncan would be to break the established laws he should obey, and the ancient customs he should observe, as the kinsman, subject and host of a monarch, whose virtuous character provides no moral warrant for killing him. Up to this point, Macbeth's mind is confined within the known parameters of his class, culture and time. But none of the prevailing religious and secular imperatives he lists, or the prohibitions they entail, are intimidating enough to deter him. The only thing that stops him in his tracks is his terror lest

> pity, like a naked new-born babe,
> Striding the blast or heaven's cherubin, horsed
> Upon the sightless couriers of the air,

Shall blow the horrid deed in every eye
That tears shall drown the wind.

$$(1.7.21–5)$$

What lends 'a naked new-born babe' such apocalyptic power is not only its capacity to personify pity and inspire compassion for the victim of murder, because its own claim on the kindness of human beings is inborn and incontestable. It is also the fact that it is the poor, bare, forked, human animal in its most unaccommodated form, not yet defined by gender, race or rank, not yet 'cabined, cribbed, confined, bound in' (3.4.23) by history and consigned to the destiny such factors dictate. It symbolizes nothing less than the latent, undefined capacity of humankind to deliver itself from its own inhumanity.

It would be hard to better the phrase 'th' milk of human[e] kindness' or the image of 'pity, like a naked new-born babe' as examples of 'the estranging language and images' through which Shakespeare's utopian vision of historical reality finds compressed expression. Echoed in such phrases as 'Ere human[e] statute purged the gentle weal' (3.4.75) and 'the sweet milk of concord' (4.3.99), and linked with the levelling imagery of blood and 'the season of all natures, sleep' (3.4.140), they define poetically the utopian ethic on whose terms Macbeth is ultimately judged, as distinct from the early modern moral code by which he stands condemned. By doing so they turn a politically conservative morality play, in which a ruthless regicidal usurper is justly destroyed, into the visionary tragedy of a medieval warlord, who makes his creed the mantra of modernity – 'for mine own good / All causes shall give way' (3.4.134–5) – and consequently butchers his way to oblivion, despite being 'too full o'th' milk of human kindness'.

Given the crucial part that phrase plays in *Macbeth*, it's not surprising to find two of the key words it enlists cropping up again in *The Tempest* at an equally crucial juncture. With his enemies completely at his mercy, Prospero is dissuaded from inflicting further retribution on them by this exchange

with Ariel, sparked by the latter's remarking, 'Your charm so
strongly works 'em / That if you now beheld them your affections / Would become tender':

Prospero   Dost thou think so, spirit?
Ariel   Mine would, sir, were I human[e].
Prospero   And mine shall.
             Hast thou, which art but air, a touch, a feeling
             Of their afflictions, and shall not myself,
             One of their kind, that relish all as sharply
             Passion as they, be kindlier moved than thou art?
                                               (5.1.17–24)

For Shakespeare, being human entails by definition the
obligation to be humane. That the obligation is ontologically
inherent in humanity is underscored by the ironic expedient
of having a discarnate being that is not human tactfully point
it out to Prospero. Implicit in the bare biological fact of
belonging to our kind, and thus possessing the same physical
faculties that allow us to 'relish all as sharply / Passion as' our
fellow human creatures, is the *a priori* moral imperative to be
as kind to them as they should be to us.

That's why pity is personified by Shakespeare as 'a naked
new-born babe': because a naked, new-born baby should
command the sympathy and care of other humans simply
by virtue of being an innocent, vulnerable, unaccommodated
creature of their own kind. Small wonder that Claudius
summons up the same image in his desperation to repent
and purge himself of the guilt of murdering his own brother:
'Bow, stubborn knees; and heart with strings of steel, / Be soft
as sinews of the new-born babe' (3.3.70–1); for it epitomizes
the unsullied state of heart and mind he might have known,
had he not been swept away by 'the corrupted currents of the
world' (3.3.57).

There's no more compelling proof of the paradoxical moral
power of helpless infancy in the whole of Shakespeare than the
proud, paternal delight Aaron takes in the bastard child his

mistress Tamora has borne him. The 'inhuman dog' (5.3.14) who casually kills the child's nurse with a vicious quip and revels, unrepentant to the last, in the countless vile atrocities he has committed, embraces his reviled black baby as 'a joyful issue' and 'a beauteous blossom' (4.2.65, 72), swearing to protect it at all costs: 'This before all the world do I prefer; / This maugre all the world will I keep safe' (4.2.108–9). When Chiron and Demetrius rebuke him for the shame brought upon them by their dark-skinned sibling, Aaron's riposte adopts the levelling line of argument this newborn baby invites – the line of argument that Shylock, Morocco and the King in *All's Well* will likewise later employ: 'He is your brother, lords, sensibly fed / Of that self blood that first gave life to you' (4.2.121–2). The psychopathic villain who brags 'like a black dog' to his torturers that he has done 'a thousand dreadful things / As willingly as one would kill a fly' (5.1.122, 141–2), prizes his vilified child above 'all the world' as 'this treasure' (4.2.172), because he perceives in the smiling 'black slave', newly 'enfranchisèd' from his mother's womb (4.2.119, 123–4), the sole repository of genuine value in the world.

A similar radical transvaluation takes place when Cleopatra cries,

> Where art thou, death?
> Come hither, come. Come, come, and take a queen
> Worth many babes and beggars.
>
> (5.2.45–7)

Cleopatra remains an imperious monarch, rating herself above all inferior mortals as a prize well worth seizing by death. As such, she enlists 'babes and beggars' as epitomes of inferiority to emphasize by contrast the full measure of her majesty. But in so doing she makes 'babes and beggars' the currency in which value is calculated; she makes the kind of human beings conventionally regarded as worth least the measure of a queen's worth. Her apostrophe of death is the subliminal trigger for the levelling impulse that links beggars and babies, and that governs the dying moments of the play. 'O eastern star!' exclaims Charmian as the venom of the asp takes hold of her mistress's life; but as before, when she insisted that she was 'No more but e'en a woman, and commanded / By such poor passion as the maid that milks / And does the meanest chores', Cleopatra rejects this grandiose appellation in favour of a more modest metaphor, in which a baby once again plays a crucial part: 'Peace, peace. / Dost thou not see my baby at my breast, / That sucks the nurse asleep?' (5.2.303–5). Death liberates Cleopatra from her royalty to enjoy, if only for a moment in her mind's eye, something far superior to royalty: the simple human bond of nurturing motherhood.

That Charmian understands this, too, is plain from the words she speaks over Cleopatra's corpse: 'Now boast thee, death, in thy possession lies / A lass unparalleled' (5.2.309–10). With that echo of her mistress's earlier apostrophe of death the inversion of the normal hierarchy of values is complete: to be an ordinary, untitled 'lass unparalleled' is to be worth more than 'a queen / Worth many babes and beggars'. So when Charmian then says, as she looks at Cleopatra's eyelids, 'Downy windows, close, / And golden Phoebus never be beheld / Of eyes again so royal' (5.2.310–12), the word 'royal' has suffered a sea-change that renders it ambivalent. It reinstates the 'lass unparalleled' as a monarch, whose crown Charmian makes a tender point of straightening on her head. But in the same breath it redefines true royalty as a quality that has nothing to do with rank, and everything to do with Cleopatra's identification of herself with 'the maid that milks / And does the meanest chores'.

The logic responsible for this inversion of conventional hierarchical values is the same as the logic that produced the gravedigger's proof that 'There is no ancient gentlemen but gardeners, ditchers and gravemakers' and Hamlet's proof that 'a king may go a progress through the guts of a beggar'. The inversion plainly does not abolish the cold fact of hierarchy in the reality that prevails both on and beyond the stage; on the contrary, it throws it into relief. But the empirical reality of hierarchy is exposed by this virtual inversion to the judgement of an imaginable human community in which neither queens nor beggars exist. 'How weak a thing is Poetry?' wrote Donne in one of his sermons, 'and yet Poetry is a counterfeit Creation, and makes things that are not, as though they were'. When Charmian says of her royal mistress, 'Now boast thee, death, in thy possession lies / A lass unparalleled', the source of the thrill the lines deliver is that through them we join that conceivable community of equals, if only for a moment, and judge the way things once were, and still are, on their utopian terms. The sublime poetic effect of Charmian's lines is the product of the play's pervasive awareness of the human potential to transform the divisive dispensation it depicts. And the mind of Cleopatra's creator is magnetically drawn to primal images of human infancy for the same reason that it's drawn to them in *Macbeth*: because the infant human being symbolizes not only the innate equality of all human beings and the equally innate potential they share at the dawn of their development, but also the moral imperative inherent in being human: the equal right of all individuals to fulfil their innate potential without detriment to the common interests of their kind.

In *The Inhuman*, his critique of the institutionalized inhumanity of global capitalism, Jean-Francois Lyotard locates the potential for resistance and transformation likewise in the native indeterminacy of childhood:

> Shorn of speech, incapable of standing upright, hesitating over the objects of its interest, not able to calculate its advantages, not sensitive to common reason, the child is eminently the human because its distress heralds and promises things possible. Its initial delay in humanity, which makes it the hostage of the adult community, is also what manifests to the community the lack of humanity it is suffering from, and which calls on it to become more human.

Writing four centuries earlier, Shakespeare enshrined the same insight far more vividly and unforgettably in the vision of 'a naked new-born babe' that flashes into the mind of a man on the brink of murdering one of his own kind. More importantly, however, in doing so he revealed the utopian possibilities embodied by that vision already emerging and taking shape at the heart of a barbaric reality.

VI

The universalizing imagination that finds stylistic expression in the wording and imagery of the plays finds structural expression, I've suggested, in the way Shakespeare pushes the polyphonic possibilities of Elizabethan drama to the limit, sharing the right of speech democratically between the diverse *dramatis personae* with scant regard for the customary proprieties, and playing havoc with hierarchy in the process. The plays' restless displacement of the dramatic perspective across a spectrum of disparate viewpoints covertly creates their *structural* identification with the *common* interests of the members of the societies they depict, rather than with one sector of those societies at the expense of the rest. But the impact of this technique is amplified by the theatrical self-consciousness of the plays, by Shakespeare's insistence on reminding us that the play we're watching is a play. I don't just mean his obvious use of the play-within-the-play device, such as 'The Mousetrap' in *Hamlet* or the farcical performance of 'Pyramus and Thisbe' in *A Midsummer Night's Dream*. I'm thinking also of his characters' habit of highlighting the fact that they are actors performing scripted roles, as when Juliet says as her death draws near, 'My dismal scene I needs must act alone' (4.3.19), or when King John realizes, in that arresting line, 'I am a scribbled form, drawn with a pen / Upon a parchment' (5.7.32–3).

I'm thinking, too, of all the disguisings, both sexual and social, to which Shakespeare repeatedly resorts, making visible the potential of these characters to be someone radically different from the person they happen to have become: Christopher Sly, 'a poor loathsome beggar' as a 'Thrice-noble lord' (Ind.1.121, Ind.2.115), Bartholomew the page as Sly's noble wife, and the servant Tranio as his master Lucentio in *The Taming of the Shrew*; Julia as the page Sebastian in *The Two Gentlemen of Verona*; Portia as the lawyer Balthazar and Nerissa as her clerk in *The Merchant of Venice*; Falstaff as 'the old woman of Brentford' in *The Merry Wives of Windsor* (4.2.77); Rosalind as Ganymede in *As You Like It* and Viola as Cesario in *Twelfth Night*; and, as we've already seen, the King of England as a common soldier at Agincourt and the son of the Earl of Gloucester as a Bedlam beggar. Like the Choruses and Prologues, the soliloquies, asides and direct addresses to the audience, which flaunt at every turn the patent artifice of the action unfolding before us, such flagrantly contrived, self-conscious dramatic devices keep the audience aware of their engrossment in an imaginary realm, where everyone and everything could have been different.

The concerted effect of these staple features of Shakespearean drama is encapsulated in remarks such as Antonio's in *The Merchant of Venice*: 'I hold the world but as the world, Gratiano – / A stage where every man must play a part' (1.1.77–9); or Duke Senior's in *As You Like It*: 'This wide and universal theatre / Presents more woeful pageants than the scene / Wherein we play in' (2.7.137–9), which explicitly calls attention to the universal perspective from which any particular scene of any particular play is implicitly perceived, and to the alternative forms and paths that people's fates can take. The effect of such remarks is to sharpen our awareness that 'All the world's a stage, / And all the men and women merely players' (2.7.139-40); or, as the motto traditionally ascribed to the Globe theatre itself puts it: '*Totus mundus agit histrionem*' or 'The whole world plays the actor'. The fact that 'All the world's a stage / And all the men and women merely players' has become an arthritic Shakespearean cliché, routinely wheeled out to sum up the transience and vanity of human life, shouldn't blind us to the subversive implications that this view of men and women and the world harbours, and that Shakespeare's drama exploits to the full.

Shakespeare's plays are intrinsically charged with the recognition that the real world is indeed like a theatre, in which people assume the identities, and perform the roles, and speak the language, and feel the desires, and live the lives, and suffer the deaths, scripted for them by the world and time in which they chance to find themselves. There's nothing fixed or immutable about the way things are in that world and time, and nothing to stop human beings assuming quite different identities, performing completely different roles, and living, loving and dying on altogether different terms under other circumstances in other kinds of society in other times. Nowhere, of course, does Shakespeare say this like that, or expressly contend through a character that such is the case. But, as I've endeavoured to demonstrate in this chapter, his plays *imply and enact* this knowledge; they articulate this understanding theatrically and poetically. In so doing they achieve what Brecht defined as the aim of all revolutionary art: they use every resource of language and theatre at their command to depict contemporary reality in such a way as to reveal that it's not the only reality possible; that how things have been until now is not how they have to be; that other forms of life are desirable and imaginable; and that men and women have had, and still have, the power to make those more desirable forms of life a reality.

If 'All the world's a stage, / And all the men and women merely players', then totally different social realities can be mounted on the stage of history, and the parts currently being played in real life, whether male or female, beggar or king, can not only be exchanged, but also superseded by roles and relationships and forms of community which have yet to be imagined, but which the universal human potential to become otherwise makes possible. That revolutionary insight may never find abstract, discursive expression in the plays, but through a host of formal, poetic and theatrical devices

Shakespeare communicates that insight in play after play with an aesthetic immediacy that no abstract, discursive statement or argument could hope to match.

Take, for example, the cross-dressed heroines of *As You Like It* and *Twelfth Night*, Rosalind and Viola, whose parts were originally played by boys, which would have made the resulting complications of identity and relationship even more bamboozling than they are in modern productions. The complications blur the boundary between male and female beyond recovery, unravelling the customary distinctions between masculine and feminine, and between homosexual and heterosexual, and creating a space beyond them in which more fluid, less repressive forms of sexual identity and desire might flourish. Thus Rosalind's assumed persona, Ganymede, provides her with a platform on which to perform her own identity as Rosalind, whom she 'pretends' to be in order to coach Orlando in the art of courtship. By detaching the character from her primary identity as exiled Duke's daughter and romantic heroine, and revealing it to be as much a role as Ganymede, Shakespeare prises open a dimension independent of both masculinity and femininity as they were then perceived, and reducible to neither. Likewise, when Rosalind finds herself wooed as a woman by Orlando, who thinks she's a man, and wooed as a beautiful youth by Phoebe, who is unaware that she's really a woman, a current of desire flows between the three characters that is impossible to define, because it keeps both heterosexual and homosexual propensities in play, defying us to tease them apart.

A similar effect is created, *mutatis mutandis*, by the web of illusion and misprision in which the identical twins Viola/Cesario and Sebastian become erotically entangled with Orsino and Olivia. But by departing from his source in making the male and female twins identical, Shakespeare pushed the boundaries even further back than he had in *As You Like It*. It's one thing to have a female character cross-dressed as a male and adrift in a zone where gender fluctuates continuously and all kinds of erotic liaisons, latent and overt, can be adumbrated. But it's quite another to make that imaginary male self a consubstantial reality in the shape of a flesh-and-blood twin brother, who supplies a *physical* solution to the heroine's romantic dilemma. In *As You Like It*, Phoebe's crush on Rosalind in the guise of Ganymede is unrequited and displaced by heterosexual wedlock with her doting swain, Silvius. But the existence of Sebastian, who conceals his real name from Olivia until after their marriage is consummated, answering happily meanwhile to 'Cesario', allows Olivia to be 'betrothed both to a maid and man' (5.1.261): to possess in Sebastian both Cesario and the Viola within Cesario. By the same token, by making his former page his 'master's mistress' (5.1.323), but never ceasing to call her 'Boy' and 'Cesario', Orsino keeps the Cesario within Viola permanently alive.

Like Montaigne, Shakespeare realized that 'both male and female, are cast in one same moulde; instruction and custom excepted, there is no great difference between them'. But he travelled imaginatively in his drama even further into the future than his fellow time-traveller in France could have dreamed of. Four hundred years ago, Shakespeare had already grasped, expressed and explored the stock assumptions and contentions of modern feminist criticism and gender theory. But he had done so in the language and theatrical vocabulary of his age, and in so doing enabled his audiences, then and now, to *envisage* far more than discursive abstraction, however prescient and enlightened, could encompass or convey. Because they are embodied and performed rather than explained and propounded, the utopian possibilities engendered by Shakespeare's transvestite imbroglios acquire a virtual reality. Brought to life through dramatized predicaments before the eyes of the audience or the mind's eye of the reader, they become viable alternatives on the verge of realization, which are utopian only in the sense that their desirability and legitimacy are *not yet* universally acknowledged. Until they are universally acknowledged, *As You Like It* and *Twelfth Night* will continue to testify to the feasibility of the *as yet* utopian by making its immanence in the actual tangible.

VII

The art that stages this fundamental conflict between the divisive constraints of the age in which Shakespeare wrote, and the universal human potential, and thus the universal human right, to live free of such indefensible constraints, is above all an art of implication. It's an art which persuades first and foremost through imagery and inference, through design and demonstration, rather than through exposition and argument. Nowhere is it more persuasive than in *A Midsummer Night's Dream*, whose 'supreme literary merit', as Chesterton shrewdly perceived, 'is a merit of design', a design that displays not only 'amazing symmetry', but also 'amazing artistic and moral beauty' in its implicit embodiment of 'a spirit that unites mankind'. What Chesterton calls, in a marvellous phrase, 'the mental hospitality and the thoughtless wisdom of Shakespeare' is expressed in *A Midsummer Night's Dream* not so much in the form of statements as in the statements of form – in the structural acts of inclusion and displacement intrinsic to the scenic architecture of the play. The concinnity of the comedy is inseparable from its 'moral beauty', its configuration of action and speech indivisible from its prefiguration of true community.

Shakespeare's previous romantic comedies had revolved around the amorous plights of their aristocratic protagonists, relegating lower-class characters to cameo roles as witty slaves or servants confined to subplots or ancillary scenes. But in this visionary play the ruling-class lovers are elbowed aside and forced to give equal room not only to supernatural creatures to whose existence they are oblivious, but also to 'rude mechanicals / That work for bread upon Athenian stalls' (3.2.9–10). This expansion of the comedic perspective to accommodate the voices, views and values of the ruled on an equal footing with their rulers creates a vision whose democratic thrust is a feat of form rather than a product of assertion. Nowhere is it stated that Theseus's presumption of omnipotence is deluded and his earthly powers subject to the sway of unearthly entities. Instead, those powers are curbed by the bewitching coda Shakespeare appends to the fifth act, dislocating the closure Theseus seems to have clinched with his valedictory couplet as the newly-weds vacate the stage: 'A fortnight hold we this solemnity / In nightly revels and new jollity' (5.1.362–3). That couplet is followed by the stage direction '*Enter Robin Goodfellow with a broom*', at which point, to quote Chesterton again, 'one touch is added which makes the play colossal'. The absolute authority assumed by Theseus is demolished not by contradiction but by formal implication, by the inferences the supplementary ending compels the spectators to draw.

Nor is this the first false ending devised by Shakespeare to subvert, through the calculated derangement of comedic form, the hierarchical assumptions that prevail within the play. Theseus exits from Act 4 with the equally conclusive couplet: 'Away with us to Athens. Three and three, / We'll hold a feast in great solemnity' (4.1.183–4). There, as far as the love-plot is concerned, the comedy might well conclude. The one remaining expectation to be satisfied is the performance of 'Pyramus and Thisbe', to house which Shakespeare manufactures a further final act. Act 5 is thus hijacked by a farcical reminder of the tragedy this comedy might have become. It's as if the vulgar, parodic jig that normally followed a performance in the public theatre had invaded the play proper, colonizing the finale normally reserved for resolving the noble protagonists' problems. *A Midsummer Night's Dream* culminates in a comic turn that allows 'Hard-handed men that work in Athens' to steal the show from the nobility, relegating them to the role of bystanders heckling from the sidelines.

The annexation of Act 5 to mount the mechanicals' unwitting spoof is the climax of a pervasive process of sly usurpation. The play consists of seven scenes: two in Athens, three in the wood, and two back in Athens. The Athenian scenes frame the sylvan scenes of erotic mayhem, which are internally framed by Quince and company's casting scene and

Bottom's reunion with his troupe. This double frame throws into relief the fact that Bottom's dalliance with Titania in Act 3 is the centrepiece of the comedy. The play's scenic structure is designed to converge on the moment when a common working man becomes the pampered consort of an adoring queen, while a queen is reduced to a tradesman's concubine and her royal spouse is cuckolded by a cloth-maker. Bully Bottom with the braying head of an ass, unfazed and completely at home in the adoring arms of the fairy queen Titania: it's the most extreme instance of social inversion, the most exquisite glimpse of hierarchy dissolved and transcended, in the whole of Shakespeare. And it's a perfect illustration of the way in which Shakespeare's drama, as Henry James observed of *The Tempest*, 'renders the poverties and obscurities of our world … in the dazzling terms of a richer and better'.

A similar effect is achieved by the long central sequence that begins in Act 2, when Titania lies down to sleep, and closes with Bottom's awakening in Act 4. That this sequence culminates in Bottom's waking to muse on his 'most rare vision', rather than the waking of Titania by Oberon or the waking of the lovers by Theseus, speaks volumes about the seditious architecture of the play. Shakespeare covertly inverts the hierarchy that prevails in the workaday world, just as he does by handing Act 5 over to the mechanicals and making Bottom's liaison with royalty the highpoint of the whole comedy. The ruler of fairyland may despise the star of 'Pyramus and Thisbe' as a 'hateful fool' (4.1.48), and the ruler of Athens may scoff at the 'tedious brief scene' (5.1.56) the craftsmen lay on for his amusement. But the formal orchestration of the play, as a medium of proleptic thought – of Shakespeare's 'thoughtless wisdom' – in its own right, holds 'sweet bully Bottom' (4.2.18) and the 'palpable-gross play' (5.1.360) performed by his 'crew of patches' (3.2.9) in higher esteem.

It's undeniable that at the end of *A Midsummer Night's Dream* male and female characters alike, the high-born and the low-born, the mortal and the immortal, remain locked inside the oppressive structures and relationships that created the conflicts the comedy strives to resolve. In that respect *A Midsummer Night's Dream*, like all Shakespeare's plays, is inextricably of its age, the irrefutable progeny of early modern English culture. But at the same time Shakespeare's poetic imagination 'bodies forth' through the medium of the drama of his day 'The forms of things unknown' (5.1.14–15), enabling things that would otherwise *not yet* be known, that could otherwise *not yet* be experienced, to materialize and be apprehended by the audience. His shaping fantasy gives 'A local habitation and a name' (5.1.14–17) to the utopian realities he could already glimpse germinating within his early modern world. As a result the audience is granted a vision even rarer than Bottom's: a vision of his world transformed into a dream of equality, a dream whose hold on the human heart remains unbroken. In this respect *A Midsummer Night's Dream*, like all Shakespeare's plays, reaches far beyond its time, and is still able to arouse in us four centuries later desires which only a radical transformation of our world will satisfy.

That's why, at this war-torn, famine-ravaged moment in history, when rapacious globalization has produced millions more 'houseless heads and unfed sides' than even Shakespeare could have imagined, and the need for distribution to undo excess that each may have enough grows more urgent every year, it matters to reclaim and activate the revolutionary significance of Shakespeare's universality and refusal to stay buried in the past. Shakespeare's bequest to us – 'what he hath left us', as Ben Jonson put it – is a truly 'wide and universal theatre' capable of granting us an extraordinary power: the power to view the past that shaped the present *as if* we already dwelt in a genuinely global community, for whom the dream of universal human equality has at last become a universal reality.

CHAPTER FOUR

'And Nothing Brings Me All Things'

I

The basic aim of this book has been twofold: to reclaim the academically taboo notion of Shakespeare's timeless universality from the conservative misconstructions that have been placed on it; and to activate the progressive interpretive possibilities his plays reveal when their timeless, universal quality is understood in a quite different sense. In developing the argument of the book, I've found my mind turning repeatedly to *Timon of Athens* – 'the strangest of Shakespeare's plays' as A. D. Nuttall rightly dubbed it – because it exemplifies, precisely by virtue of its strangeness and ostensible eccentricity among his works, the quintessential qualities that account for their enduring power and importance. The standpoint from which all Shakespeare's plays are shaped and worded can be seen in its starkest, most uncompromising form in *Timon of Athens*. So I want to conclude with a reading of *Timon* designed to recapitulate the argument of the book, but in a way that seeks to do justice to the profound estrangement of Shakespeare's plays – at times violent and pitiless, at times compassionately, playfully ironic – from the world and time they dramatized in a host of different guises.

As I've endeavoured to demonstrate in the previous chapters, the perspective that Shakespeare forged through language and form as he wrote, and from which he depicted life in his era with such electrifying immediacy, is the mainspring of his drama's ability to transcend its time while transcribing its time, to be at once the 'Soul of the age' in which he wrote and yet 'not of an age, but for all time'. Possessed as he wrote by 'the prophetic soul / Of the wide world dreaming on things to come', Shakespeare appraised his epoch with the eyes of a man steeped in the culture and language of that epoch, but deeply alienated from it by his anticipation of the day 'When earthly things made even / Atone together' (*As You Like It*, 5.4.107–8) and human beings are united at last as one in a just society.

With his customary acuity, Coleridge latched onto this fundamental detachment of Shakespeare's creative imagination, capturing it perfectly when he wrote of *Venus and Adonis*: 'Shakespeare works exactly in this poem *as if he were of another planet*, with perfect abstraction from himself' (my italics). The supreme quality Coleridge discerns in the poem is 'the alienation, and, if I may hazard the expression, the utter *aloofness* of the poet's own feelings, from those of which he is at once the painter and the analyst'. That strange, alienated quality attracts comments from Coleridge again when he muses on Shakespeare's inexplicability in terms of his time and astutely traces it to the idiosyncratic way he uses words, to the fact that 'His language is entirely his own': 'The construction of Shakespeare's sentences, whether in verse or prose, is the necessary and homogeneous vehicle of his peculiar manner of thinking. His is not the style of the age.' So when we read the plays, as Coleridge reflects elsewhere, 'we are aware that they are not of our age', because they are self-evidently the products of an earlier age; yet 'in one sense they may be said to be of no age':

A friend of mine well remarked of Spenser that he is out of space; the reader never knows where he is, but still he knows, from the consciousness within him, that all is as natural and proper as if the country where the action is laid were distinctly pointed out, and marked down in a map. Shakespeare is as much out of time as Spenser is out of space ...

Coleridge comes closer than most here to describing Shakespeare's simultaneous reflection of and remoteness from all that seemed 'natural and proper' to his era. The reason why his plays 'may be said to be of no age' in one sense – because what Sir Philip Sidney called 'the universal consideration' is built into them – lies beyond Coleridge's grasp. But the fact that they are written in a manner and a frame of mind that lifts them 'out of time', in the sense that their anchorage in their age alone can't begin to account for them, does not escape him.

Nor did it escape Thomas Hardy a century later in the poem he addressed in 1916 'To Shakespeare: After Three Hundred Years', assuring his mighty precursor that he could count on remaining 'at heart unread eternally' thanks to his 'strange mind'. Like Coleridge, Hardy was responding to a quality at the heart of Shakespeare's works that remained enigmatic centuries after his death, because it defied complete explication in the terms of the past or the present. And no critical or theatrical response to the plays will get very far if it doesn't begin by recognizing the strangeness of Shakespeare's creative intelligence, the alien 'aloofness' of his attitude to his material, which does indeed make him seem 'as if he were of another planet'. That planet, I've been arguing, is our own planet in the transfigured future Shakespeare's drama could foreshadow, because the human potential and the human need to forge such a future could already be sensed everywhere around him, and they found expression in every tale he told through the way he told it.

'It is with the future that we have to deal', observes Oscar Wilde in 'The Soul of Man under Socialism'. 'For the past is what man should not have been. The present is what man ought not to be. The future is what artists are.' Once one grasps Shakespeare's imaginative alienation as a denizen of futurity marooned in the past, all kinds of things in his plays become clearer, and clues to the viewpoint from which they are penned become apparent everywhere. If that viewpoint is incarnate anywhere in the plays, it's in the mercurial figure of the wise fool, who plainly held a special fascination for his creator. Shakespeare's fully-fledged professional fools, Touchstone, Feste and the nameless fool of Lear, participate in the events and exchanges of their plays, yet are curiously detached from them; they inhabit the same fictive universe and timescape as the rest of the cast, yet they dwell simultaneously apart from them in the space and time occupied by whichever audience is watching them, as the cryptic prophecy of a prophecy uttered by the fool in *King Lear* makes uncannily clear.

Of the role of the fool in Shakespeare, Coleridge remarked: 'We meet with characters who are, as it were, unfeeling spectators of the most passionate situations, constantly in life. The Fool serves to supply the place of some such uninterested person where all the characters besides have interest.' Coleridge had Lear's fool in particular in mind, but John Middleton Murry, employing the same word Coleridge used of *Venus and Adonis*, detected the same 'strange aloofness in Feste'. Attached to nobody, 'He is woven in and out the play like a careless wraith' and his fooling 'is almost metaphysical in its aloofness'. It is indeed, because Feste embodies the transhistorical elevation from which not only Shakespearean comedy but also Shakespearean drama in general is written. He is disinterested and attached to nobody in *Twelfth Night*, because he doesn't belong to the world and time of the play through which he's passing. As a rootless revenant from a future purged of the conflicts that warped the minds and lives of early modern English men and women, he speaks in the name of a human community that has yet to come into being. That's why he speaks in the incorrigibly ironic, riddling dialect, designed to be dismissed as nonsense by his baffled interlocutors, that sets Shakespeare's wise fools apart. That's why this formidable anachronism, the spirit of humanity adrift in a world that has no home for it yet, can step out of the time frame of *Twelfth Night* and into the audience's, and place the whole play in a vast temporal continuum, which stretches back from the present moment of performance – whenever that may be – to the moment when 'A great while ago the world begun'.

By his very presence in a work of literature, as Bakhtin observes, the figure of the wise fool 'makes strange the world of social conventionality', because he has 'the right to be "other" in this world, the right not to make common cause with any single one of the existing categories that life makes available'. The obvious relish with which Shakespeare lets Feste, Touchstone and Lear's fool off the leash to play fast and loose with language and logic owes more than a little to the character's kinship with his creator. The figure of the licensed fool resonates so strongly with Shakespeare, because as a dramatist he claims and exercises the same right to expose the inhuman strangeness of the social conventions – 'the plague of custom' (*King Lear*, 1.2.3) – that constricted life in his time; the same right 'not to make common cause with any single one of the existing categories that life makes available', which are at odds with the common cause of humanity.

Thus the motley-minded playwright, who created in the licensed fool an avatar of the dramatist who dreamt him up, would have had no trouble dreaming up Barnardine, the impassive convict on death row who, as Hazlitt perceived, holds the key to the vision of *Measure for Measure*. 'A man that apprehends death no more dreadfully but as a drunken sleep; careless, reckless, and fearless of what's past, present or to come' (4.2.144–6), supremely indifferent to punishment and pardon alike, Barnardine is the Duke's injunction to 'Be absolute for death' (3.1.5) made flesh. In the shambling guise of Barnardine we behold not merely, in Hazlitt's words, 'a fine antithesis to the morality and hypocrisy of the other characters of the play', but the embodiment of the play's dispassionate attitude to everything that matters so vitally to everyone imprisoned in its plot.

In the ethereal figure of Ariel, moreover, Shakespeare creates, as was noted in the last chapter, a being who views the situation in *The Tempest* from a position outside humanity altogether; in fact, he populates the whole island with disembodied non-human beings,

> Who though they are of monstrous shape, yet note
> Their manners are more gentle-kind than of
> Our human generation you shall find
> Many, nay, almost any.

> (3.3.31–4)

This accolade is delivered, aptly enough, by the utopian dreamer Gonzalo, in whose ideal commonwealth all things would be executed by contraries. A decade and a half earlier, however, in the comedy whose core story sprang like *The Tempest*'s entirely from its author's imagination, Shakespeare had already gone even further in his creation of the fairies in *A Midsummer Night's Dream*. Although the effect of their manipulation of the lovers' fate is ultimately benign, they remain inscrutably alien creatures, 'spirits of another sort' (3.3.389), whose exact origin, nature and aims are unfathomable, and whose attitude to 'human mortals' (2.1.101) is bemusement at the behaviour of an inferior species: 'Lord, what fools these mortals be!' (3.2.115). The point being that Shakespeare invites us to share that Olympian attitude. We alone, along with Bottom, have been privileged to behold the alien beings responsible for the resolution, and to understand, unlike all the human characters including Bottom, how the final state of 'gentle concord' (4.1.142) has been brought about. Shakespeare makes visible and explicable to the audience what remains invisible and inexplicable to the human *dramatis personae*. In so doing he distances the audience from the human world as it stands, propelling us beyond the orbit of human experience and comprehension in

his time to a point from which we can look back down upon
our kind as if we no longer belonged to it.

This drive to disengage and draw back, this constant quest
for positions on the periphery, or beyond the boundary, of
human life as it happened to be in his day is a fundamental
feature of Shakespeare's dramatic art. It's what accounts for
his compulsive leaps from the past or present into the future;
his mental vaults back to the beginning of the world when
Adam delved, or forward to doomsday and the dissolution of
this great globe itself; his instinctive reaching for the image of
the innocent new-born child on the threshold of its thraldom
to history; his recurrent resort to the absolute detachment
of death and life viewed from the grave; his attraction to
outsiders and exiles, to the dispossessed, the deranged, the
forlorn and the ostracized; and his imaginative empathy not
only with figures reviled as inhuman, but also with beings
who are not human at all. Indeed, one can sense the fleeting
deployment of distance in the very use of the word 'human':
when Rosalind, for example, masquerading as Ganymede,
promises to set the real Rosalind before Orlando's eyes the
next day, 'human as she is' (*As You Like It*, 5.2.65); when
Coriolanus is said to regard the plebs 'in human action and
capacity' (2.2.246) as mere beasts of burden; or when Paulina
dismisses the notion that Leontes's lost child might be found
as 'monstrous to our human reason' (*The Winter's Tale*,
5.1.41). In each of these and many other instances, including
those discussed in the last chapter, the word pulls us back for
a moment to the subliminal standpoint of the play itself. And
in Shakespeare's original spelling – 'humane' – it secretes in
each instance a tacit moral judgement of humanity as it is by
humanity as it should be.

We're subconsciously pulled back even further for a second
when Oberon assures Titania that 'We the globe can compass
soon' (*A Midsummer Night's Dream*, 4.1.96); when Hal calls
Falstaff 'thou globe of sinful continents' (*2 Henry IV*, 2.4.288);
when Hamlet speaks of 'this distracted globe' (1.5.97) and
Othello of 'th'affrighted globe' (5.2.109); or when Ulysses

evokes the apocalyptic image of the oceans engulfing their shores to 'make a sop of all this solid globe' (*Troilus and Cressida*, 1.3.113). The same sensation is produced by Juliet's likening of Romeo's brow to 'a throne where honour may be crowned / Sole monarch of the universal earth' (3.1.93–4); by the Chorus's description of Henry V's 'liberal eye' dispensing 'A largess universal, like the sun' (4.Chorus.43–4); by Malcolm's feigning a desire to 'Uproar the universal peace, confound / All unity on earth' (*Macbeth*, 4.3.101–2); and by the Third Gentleman's reporting of the reunion of Leontes with Perdita, 'If all the world could have seen't, the woe had been universal' (5.2.90–1).

The effect of such lines, however brief and discreet it may be, is best explained by quoting those pregnant lines of Duke Senior's once more and bearing their context in mind:

> Thou seest we are not all alone unhappy.
> This wide and universal theatre
> Presents more woeful pageants than the scene
> Wherein we play in.
>
> (*As You Like It*, 2.7.136–9)

From a close-up on the plight of Orlando, which prompts the Duke to this reflection, we suddenly zoom out and see it from a 'wide and universal' perspective. This particular sad scenario, on which the play is focusing at this point, is placed in the global context of all the other 'woeful pageants' other human beings are bound to be acting out elsewhere. The *theatrum mundi* topos, in whose terms the speech is couched, stresses the contingency of whatever pageant human beings happen to find themselves cast in, wherever in the world they happen to be. The Duke's speech concisely illustrates, in other words, the indivisibility of Shakespeare's detached, universal perspective from his awareness of the human potential to be otherwise, for better and for worse, than the circumstances in any given place and time dictate.

I've no wish to overstate the significance of these uses of the words 'human', 'globe' and 'universal', or of Shakespeare's equally resonant uses of the words 'world', 'earth', 'man', 'kind' and 'common'. But they do provide further corroboration of Shakespeare's hard-wired tendency to write at an extreme remove from the ethos of the early modern era. That tendency is the product not of Shakespeare's indifference to the current fate of his fellow men and women, but of his commitment to the future emancipation of humanity. It's because he perceives so clearly in his plays the innate equality and universal potentiality of human beings that the vision of his plays is so profoundly estranged from Renaissance reality. Or perhaps it would be more accurate to say that the price of his drama's utopian identification with humanity as it could be is its fundamental alienation from the state of humanity in his time.

The play in which Shakespeare comes closest to staging his own tragic plight as a dramatist is unquestionably *Timon of Athens*, one of the few plays, as Hazlitt observes, 'in which he seems to be in earnest throughout, never to trifle nor go out of his way', never to let the intensity of feeling flag. For Wilson Knight, who regarded *Timon of Athens* as 'preeminent among the tragedies', the reason for its relentless earnestness and intensity was plain: 'Shakespeare, to put it bluntly, wanted for once to speak out and unburden his soul.' Knight, not surprisingly, has incurred the mockery of most Shakespearean critics for putting it that bluntly, and for according an evidently unfinished play, parts of which turned out to have been written by Middleton, such preeminence in the canon. But the mockery is undeserved because, unlike most Shakespearean critics, Knight rightly sensed that *Timon of Athens* is a paradigmatic play, which distils the essence of Shakespeare's dramatic vision, rather than a bizarre, abortive aberration. His claim that 'Timon is man's futurity, what man must measure himself by in order to advance' might well seem baffling at first sight, but from the standpoint of the argument of this book, as I hope to show, it makes perfect sense. Whether Knight was correct to surmise that 'Shakespeare, fearing its boldness, left the play unrevised' must remain a matter for conjecture. But his critical instincts were never surer than when he wrote: 'Probably the prophetic nature of the play has something to do with its faults, if they be faults. Shakespeare may have put it aside prematurely, thinking it a failure, though the truth is that he was writing before his time, and almost out of his depth.' And he was writing almost out of his depth because, as Knight intuitively perceives, *Timon of Athens* 'overspans, and outspans, the centuries'.

II

The vantage point from which *Timon of Athens* is imagined is brought sharply into focus by Shakespeare's obsession with Timon's epitaph. (My account of the play, needless to say, is anchored in the lion's share of the lines that recent scholarship has credited to Shakespeare.) When the cynical philosopher Apemantus locks horns in the woods with Timon, whose overnight mutation into *Misanthropos* he suspects of being an affectation, a blatant aping of his own professional posture, he says to Timon, 'Thou shouldst desire to die, being miserable'. 'Not by his breath that is more miserable' (4.3.249–50), retorts Timon, disdaining to take instruction from someone who would have been 'a knave and flatterer' (4.3.277) like those he excoriates, if low birth and adversity hadn't prevented him. But within a hundred lines of this acerbic exchange Timon intimates that Apemantus's scepticism about his death-wish will prove as misconceived as his allegation that Timon is merely impersonating a misanthropist. Turning from Apemantus, Timon addresses himself in a speech that sounds like a soliloquy:

> I am sick of this false world, and will love naught
> But even the mere necessities upon't.
> Then, Timon, presently prepare thy grave.
> Lie where the light foam of the sea may beat

Thy gravestone daily. Make thine epitaph,
That death in me at others' lives may laugh.

(4.3.378–83)

Then he switches abruptly from apostrophizing himself to apostrophizing the gold he has unearthed, in one of the passages that Marx found so germane to his critique of capitalism:

O, thou sweet king-killer, and dear divorce
'Twixt natural son and sire; thou bright defiler
Of Hymen's purest bed; thou valiant Mars;
Thou ever young, fresh, loved, and delicate wooer,
Whose blush doth thaw the consecrated snow
That lies on Dian's lap; thou visible god,
That sold'rest close impossibilities
And mak'st them kiss, that speak'st with every tongue
To every purpose. O thou touch of hearts:
Think thy slave man rebels, and by thy virtue
Set them into confounding odds, that beasts
May have the world in empire.

(4.3.384–95)

This speech contains the first allusion to Timon's grave and epitaph, which he locates in his mind's eye at the ever-shifting border between land and sea, and thus in an eternal, diurnal zone beyond the jurisdiction of 'Old Time the clock-setter, that bald sexton Time' invoked by the Bastard in *King John* (3.1.250). Here we have, too, in Timon's envisaging of his inscribed gravestone, the first foreshadowing of the posthumous standpoint he is now impatient to adopt. The retrospective view of the living enshrined in Timon's epitaph will find expression in laughter, which will allow him to mock humanity *post mortem*, and delight in the liberty from their risible fate the grave has granted him. That death as universal leveller as well as liberator is lurking in these lines, and graphically implicit in the image of the gravestone, is confirmed by the first phrase of his apostrophe to the gold: 'O, thou sweet king-killer'. Timon's mind moves instinctively from the prospect of a contemptuous perspective on his kind to lauding the power of money to buy the murder of a monarch, the epitome of the unequal distribution of wealth and power on which the 'false world', from which death alone can deliver Timon, depends. It does so because Timon's apostrophe to himself and his apostrophe to gold are linked by the same covert logic.

To put it simply, Timon's ironic eulogy of the pernicious virtues of gold *explains* why he is 'sick of this false world' and craves the release of death: the omnipotent, ubiquitous sway of money is the root cause of his implacable misanthropy and moribund state. But the irony is complex, and not just compromised but at times undermined, by the passionately laudatory terms in which the mock encomium is couched. The 'king-killer' is 'sweet'; the 'divorce / 'Twixt natural son and sire' is 'dear'; the 'defiler / Of Hymen's purest bed' is 'bright' and 'valiant' like the adulterous Mars; the defiler of chastity is an 'ever young, fresh, loved and delicate wooer'. Up to this point, the instances are such as to sustain the ironic effect a satirical misanthropist might be expected to seek. But it's harder to read the ensuing lines as equivocal in the absence of comparable cases of despicable conduct to undercut the praise:

>   thou visible god,
> That sold'rst close impossibilities
> And mak'st them kiss, that speak'st with every tongue
> To every purpose; O thou touch of hearts …

In fact, it's hard to construe this part of Timon's paean to the universal potency of money as pejorative at all; on the contrary, the capacity to make impossibilities kiss, to speak in the interests of every human being, and to touch the human heart in the sense of testing its mettle as well as in the sense of moving it, seem to be attributes as desirable as they are admirable.

These lines can't be isolated, of course, from their context in a speech that praises gold for financing murder and immorality, and that concludes by exhorting it to incite human beings to destroy each other. But they point to a more profound ambiguity about the power of money in *Timon of Athens*. Timon's panegyric may be governed by his prayer to gold to contrive the extinction of the species; but his erotically charged empathy with the violations bought by the 'visible god', the rapturous language he employs in its praise, the universalizing thrust of his rhetoric, and the global scale of his vision betray a recognition on the part of the play, if not the character, that more may be at stake in money than meets the misanthropic eye.

Let me park that point there for the moment and turn to Timon's next allusion to his epitaph, which concludes his first refusal to succumb to the Senators' plea that he save Athens from the wrath of Alcibiades. 'Why', muses Timon half to himself, having taken mocking leave of them:

> I was writing of my epitaph.
> It will be seen tomorrow. My long sickness
> Of health and living now begins to mend
> And nothing brings me all things.

(5.2.70–3)

The last sentence sounds like an epitaph itself, uttered from beyond the grave. The writing of the actual epitaph is inseparable from the anticipated future in which the living will read it. The shift from the past continuous to the future tense in the first two lines underscores this; so does the fact that, after the tense shifts again to the present in the following line, mooring Timon for a moment in the immediate 'now', it leaps forward again, this time into the proleptic present tense, with the startling statement 'And nothing brings me all things': a line which evokes the ineffable plenitude of oblivion Timon expects death to grant him as if he *already* enjoys it.

That line has obvious affinities with other uses of the word 'nothing' in other plays, including: 'Nothing almost sees miracles / But misery' (2.2.156–7) and 'Edgar I nothing am' (2.2.184), to cite just two of the many instances in *King Lear*; the 'airy nothing' to which 'the poet's pen' gives 'A local habitation and a name' in *A Midsummer Night's Dream* (5.1.15–17); 'He was a kind of nothing, titleless' (5.1.13), which is Cominius's comment on Coriolanus's refusal to answer to any name; and, closest in spirit to Timon's line, Richard II's 'Nor I, nor any man that but man is, / With nothing shall be pleased till he be eased / With being nothing' (5.5.39–41). All these quotations attest, like Timon's line, to the truth of Middleton Murry's observation that in Shakespeare's plays 'it is possible that a nothingness may be more real than a character, just as our unknown selves in life are sometimes more potent than our known'. In no other instance of its use in Shakespeare, as far as I'm aware, is 'nothing' employed as it is in Timon's line to signify complete, serene fulfilment. Even in those lines of Richard's the annihilation of the socially conditioned self is seen as a merciful release from suffering rather than greeted as the blissful apotheosis of human existence. But Murry's inspired insight identifies the reason why so many of Shakespeare's otherwise disparate uses of the term resonate so strongly with each other across the canon. Nothingness assumes for Shakespeare a paradoxical solidity and power, which can make it seem more real than a known, recognizable character, when it connotes the unknown, as yet unrealized potential of people and circumstances to be absolutely different from, and thus absolutely free from, what historical happenstance has decreed that they must be. And nowhere in the plays is there a line that makes sheer potentiality, the absolute antithesis of the actual, more thrillingly palpable than Timon's line 'And nothing brings me all things'.

Thirty lines later, having teased the craven Senators with the hope that he'll relent, Timon returns to his obsession with this dismissive valediction:

Come not to me again, but say to Athens,
Timon hath made his everlasting mansion
Upon the beachèd verge of the salt flood,
Who once a day with his embossèd froth
The turbulent surge shall cover. Thither come,
And let my gravestone be your oracle.
Lips, let four words go by, and language end.
What is amiss, plague and infection mend.
Graves only be men's works, and death their gain,
Sun, hide thy beams. Timon hath done his reign.

(5.2.99–108)

With that, he exits the stage, never to reappear. Note again the stress on the grave as an '*everlasting* mansion', subject only to the endless, non-human rhythms of sun, moon and tide, as distinct from the time-bound life 'that this brief world affords' (4.3.254), which Timon will soon have left behind. Note, too, that the hitherto latent linking of the gravestone and its epitaph to the posthumous future ('It will be seen tomorrow') becomes patent as the gravestone morphs into an oracle, a cryptic predictor of the future.

In one sense, of course, there's nothing cryptic to decipher: the Athenians who visit Timon's grave will behold in the tombstone an earnest of their own mortal fate. But in another sense the enigmatic nature of the epitaph is crucial to its vatic effect, as the very next line, with its distinctly oracular ring, suggests: 'Lips, let four words go by, and language end.' The arbitrary specificity of '*four* words' has had editors tying themselves in knots to provide a logical explanation or justify emending the original text. But the arbitrary specificity is precisely what lends the line its strange potency as an apocalyptic curse, which needs no more emending than the riddling maledictions of the witches in *Macbeth*. Moreover, the randomness of 'let four words go by' accentuates the abruptness of the moment in which language, and thus the whole social formation it sustains, is envisaged as ceasing to exist. From Timon's intransigent standpoint the complicity of language in perpetuating the status quo is fundamental and unforgivable, as the earlier imprecation with which he had greeted the Senators makes plain:

> Speak and be hanged.
> For each true word a blister, and each false
> Be as a cantherizing to the root o'th' tongue,
> Consuming it with speaking.
>
> (5.2.16–19)

That the master dramatist of his day could voice through Timon such unmitigated contempt for the medium of his own art speaks volumes about Shakespeare's capacity for disengaging himself emotionally and imaginatively from everything that passed for life at the dawn of the seventeenth century.

The *actual* epitaph, when the first of its three versions is finally revealed within 20 lines of Timon's last exit, turns out to be as puzzling as the line 'let my gravestone be your oracle' might lead one to expect. In a scene occupying a mere ten lines, a scene routinely omitted in performance, a nameless soldier seeking Timon in the woods discovers his inscribed tomb:

> What is this?
> 'Timon is dead, who hath outstretched his span.
> Some beast read this; there does not live a man.'
> Dead, sure, and this his grave. What's on this tomb
> I cannot read. The character I'll take with wax.
> Our captain hath in every figure skill,
> An aged interpreter, though young in days.
>
> (5.4.2–8)

The second line of the inscription has taxed the ingenuity of some of the best aged interpreters *de nos jours*. It's clearly, first and foremost, an insult primed to explode in the face of future readers of the epitaph: 'If you're reading this, you must be a beast.' The sarcastic syllogism on which the insult tacitly rests is: 'Only humans can read; all humans are beasts; therefore a beast is reading this.' The sentence 'there does not live a man' tilts the line into a different light, however, striking a note of lamentation: 'Some beast is going to have to read this, because there's no creature living that merits the name of man.' And that plainly presupposes a conception of what human beings are capable of becoming, but have so far failed to become. But the imperative 'Some beast read this' also secretes a statement in the optative mood. It's a wish, an expression of desire, as much as a command: '*May* some beast read this' or '*Let* some beast read this'. As such, it invites us to construe the statement 'there does not live a man' as another resort to the proleptic present: as Timon's anticipation of the post-human era to which he adverted in his prayer to gold, the invisible god, to set human beings 'into confounding odds, that beasts / May have the world in empire'. A paraphrase of the line thus construed might be: 'May the time come when there are only beasts left to read this, because humanity is extinct.'

Much editorial ink has been spilt over the soldier's saying 'What's on this tomb / I cannot read', because he has just read the epitaph out. But there's no need to regard it as a contradiction requiring radical surgery (*The Oxford Shakespeare* cuts the epitaph completely) or elaborate explication. In the Crystals' glossary *Shakespeare's Words* the first meaning given for 'read' is 'interpret', a meaning that reaches back to the word's Anglo-Saxon roots and survives in ordinary modern usage – when we speak, for example, of reading the expression on someone's face or providing a reading of a text. Assuming, then, that this is the sense of the word intended here, the soldier is simply saying, 'I don't understand what that means'. This inference is borne out most obviously by the soldier's having just demonstrated his literacy by reading the epitaph aloud, but also by his resolving to take a wax impression of the epitaph to an experienced 'interpreter', who will explain the import of the couplet the soldier has read but not understood.

The main aspect of this scene I want to highlight, however, is the way the posthumous point of view and the oracular inscription on the gravestone both reach into the future beyond the moment in which they were forged: the posthumous viewpoint by exploiting in life the retrospective licence of death; the epitaph by engendering a process of interpretation that will continue long after the epitaphs of Timon's most recent editors have been written. In these twin respects Timon's virtual and actual epitaphs enshrine essential qualities of Shakespeare's dramatic vision throughout his career, a vision in which the posthumous perspective and the obligation to interpret are inextricable.

They are certainly inextricable in the final epitaph, or rather pair of epitaphs, bequeathed to us by the First Folio. Immediately after Alcibiades has been dissuaded from laying Athens waste, the anonymous soldier enters again and addresses him:

> My noble general, Timon is dead,
> Entombed upon the very hem o'th' sea;
> And on his gravestone this insculpture, which
> With wax I brought away, whose soft impression
> Interprets for my poor ignorance.

(5.5.66–70)

Once again it's the *interpretation* of the 'insculpture', not the basic ability to read what it says, that's at issue. But the soldier's faith in Alcibiades' credentials as 'An aged interpreter' proves to have been misplaced, when the latter merely reads the carved inscription out and leaves the problem it poses to perplex future editors:

> Here lies a wretched corpse,
>   Of wretched soul bereft.
> Seek not my name. A plague consume
>   You wicked caitiffs left!
> Here lie I, Timon, who alive

All living men did hate.
Pass by and curse thy fill, but pass
And stay not here thy gait.

(5.5.71–8)

Not only is this epitaph quite different from the one the soldier had earlier read out, but it's composed of two epitaphs lifted from Shakespeare's principal source, Plutarch, where the first couplet is credited to Timon and the second to the poet Callimachus. The problem, of course, is the glaring contradiction between 'Seek not my name' in the first epitaph and 'Here lie I, Timon' in the second one. This contradiction has led some editors to delete the first couplet on the assumption that Shakespeare (or possibly Middleton) must have intended but failed to cancel one of them; and, in the same misconceived quest for logical consistency, productions usually follow suit, as well as ditching the earlier scene in which the soldier reads a different epitaph from the one Alcibiades reads. But, even if these apparent inconsistencies and contradictions could be credibly explained as the results of authorial error or oversight, their disconcerting impact is entirely congruous with the recalcitrant spirit and experimental form of the play, and they should be left to stand instead of airbrushed away by meddling editors and directors. As Stephen Dedalus observes of Shakespeare in the Scylla and Charybdis episode of *Ulysses*: 'A man of genius makes no mistakes. His errors are volitional and are the portals of discovery.'

III

The epitaphs in *Timon of Athens* are indeed portals of discovery, through which we can perceive more clearly than in any other play the main concerns and key features of Shakespeare's dramatic art. Their posthumous standpoint epitomizes the proleptic trajectory of that art, its impatience with the age it portrayed. The cast of mind that left its imprint in the form and language of the plays drove their author to dramatize life in his time as if it already belonged to a past that no longer shackled him. Nadine Gordimer once remarked, 'in my fiction I am writing as if I were dead', her reason being that writing 'as if your writing is posthumous' grants an author 'absolute freedom': absolute freedom from the assumptions and commitments, the inhibitions and constraints, that would otherwise hobble the author's imagination, locking it inside the world and time from which it seeks total detachment. With this desideratum in mind, Timon's fixation on cryptic epitaphs looks less like the morbid eccentricity of a deranged misanthrope – although it's obviously that too – and more like a transposed authorial obsession, which acquires its resonance from being tuned to the frequency of Shakespeare's imagination. When Coleridge hailed Shakespeare as 'the great, ever living, dead man', the posthumous author *par excellence*, he spoke more truly than he realized.

The appeal that this implacable misanthropist and his craving for oblivion held for Shakespeare becomes less difficult to fathom, once the play's intimate bearing on its author's creative disposition becomes apparent. The absolute freedom on which Gordimer predicates the creation of fiction is a freedom which the virtual dispensation of death alone can grant. In Shakespeare's case, complete, disinterested detachment from the place and time in which one lives not only opens his dramatic vision up to the future, but also grounds it in the democracy of the dead, whose absolute liberty the living are cruelly denied. Robert Southey's poem 'My days among the dead are passed' captures memorably the convergence of death, hope, desire and the future in the posthumous imagination:

> My hopes are with the dead, anon
> My place with them will be,
> And I with them shall travel on
> Through all futurity.

The utopian overtones of these lines find an amplified echo in Wallace Stevens' poem 'Sunday Morning':

Death is the mother of beauty; hence from her,
Alone, shall come fulfilment to our dreams
And our desires.

Re-read in the light of these quotations from Southey and Stevens, the utopian tenor of Timon's valediction to the Senators becomes visible: 'My long sickness / Of health and living now begins to mend, / And nothing brings me all things.' If there's a tragedy at the heart of this unclassifiable play, it's that the fulfilment of the dreams and desires of Shakespeare's time is so remote that it can be imagined only in a state from which humanity in its present form has been purged, a state symbolized by, if not synonymous with, death – death devoid of the promise of redemption in a Christian heaven. By the same token, however, the posthumous perspective serves to keep the prospect of the transformation of human life alive in the present.

For Bakhtin, 'the essence of Shakespeare's world consciousness', the secret of his universality and global appeal, is the 'belief in the possibility of a complete exit from the present order of this life' that pervades his plays. A complete exit from the present order of this life is, of course, precisely what Timon of Athens yearns for and achieves through death. Timon's utter misanthropic disenchantment with the world as it is constitutes the most extreme instance of the attitude that ultimately animates all Shakespeare's drama. It's a measure of Shakespeare's empathy with his protagonist that Timon's disillusionment with his kind embraces not only the Poet and the Painter, the mercenary incarnations of literature and art who open the play, but also the play's own lifeblood, language itself, whose complicity in sustaining the inhuman status quo condemns it to eradication. Nor would Timon's exit from the prevailing social dispensation be complete without his shuffling off time along with his mortal coil, since as long as human beings remain incarcerated in the prison house of time, the ways of life which that temporal fiction was devised to serve will continue to control their hearts and minds. That's why Timon is so adamant that his grave be sited at the point where the ocean eternally laps the shore in a dimension beyond the reach of time; and why Alcibiades reinforces the timelessness of Timon's posthumous vantage point in the speech with which he closes the play: 'Though thou abhorred'st in us our human griefs', he says, addressing the dead man as if he were alive and present, 'yet rich conceit / Taught thee to make vast Neptune weep for aye / On thy low grave' (5.5.80, 83–4).

Why is Shakespeare so fascinated by a figure who projects himself beyond death into a future unfettered by time and free of everything, including language, that previously defined him as a human being of his day? It's because that projected realm provides a privileged imaginative space, a subjunctive domain, in which the concept of common humanity subsists, and in which a universal point of view can be adopted and brought to bear on the brutally divisive, ruthlessly acquisitive society that surrounds him. That's what empowers his plays to depict the terms on which people lived 400 years ago from a standpoint that's still so far in advance of the consensus of our time that they can take the measure of the brutally divisive, ruthlessly acquisitive society that still surrounds us more effectively than any modern play has managed to. Shakespearean drama is 'time*less*' insofar as it invites us to experience events within time as if we dwelt beyond time as human society has so far known it, in a realm of pure, as yet unfulfilled potentiality: the realm Timon calls the 'nothing' that will bring him 'all things', because it will be the negation of everything that has denied individuals their inalienable human right to fulfil their potential in ways that also serve the interests of the human community as a whole.

What's so troubling about *Timon of Athens* is precisely the fact that this utopian perspective is articulated primarily, although by no means exclusively, through negation rather than affirmation. What Robert Weimann calls 'the universalizing and humanizing effect of Shakespeare's dramaturgy' is mainly achieved in *Timon of Athens* through Timon's protracted howl of rage at a society shamelessly inured to the heartless individualism that sacrifices the shared interests of its members to rabid self-interest, that 'Smells from the general weal', as Timon pungently puts it, in its lust for 'particular' profit (4.3.159–60). The moment Timon's volteface from selfless philanthropy to vicious misanthropy is announced by the stage direction '*Enter Timon, in a rage*', he perceives his plight as involving the whole of humanity: 'The place which I have feasted,' cries Timon, 'does it now, / Like all mankind, show me an iron heart?' (3.4.83–4). From that moment on, the universalizing rhetoric is relentless: 'Henceforth hated be / Of Timon man and all humanity!' (3.7.103–4); 'And grant, as Timon grows, his hate may grow / To the whole race of mankind, high and low' (4.1.39–40); 'Therefore be abhorred / All feasts, societies, and throngs of men' (4.3.20–1); 'damnèd earth, / Thou common whore of mankind' (4.3.42–3); 'Common mother – thou / Whose womb immeasurable and infinite breast / Feeds all' (4.3.178–80); 'All that you meet are thieves. To Athens go, / Break open shops; nothing can you steal / But thieves do lose it' (4.3.448–50); 'One that rejoices in the common wrack / As common bruit doth put it' (5.2.77–8); and so on, until death silences him and only his epitaph is left to attest to his comprehensive loathing.

The whole of humanity is kept in focus on a global, indeed cosmic scale, even as Timon reviles it. We're constantly compelled to view and judge the values that ruled Shakespeare's world from a collective vantage point outside that world, beyond the reach of hierarchy, systemic selfishness, and the endemic alienation of what Ben Jonson dubbed 'the money-get, mechanic age'. The ferocity of Timon's misanthropic tirades reveals how deeply, indeed terminally wounded he is by the failure of his kind to act according to the principles of kindness that it's manifestly capable of conceiving and of living by. Every tirade vindicates *ex negativo* the ideals of equality, mutuality and community, and the human potential to achieve them, that are betrayed by the organized enslavement of human beings to the pursuit of profit by the few to the detriment of the many. No work of literature testifies more eloquently than *Timon of Athens* to the truth of Adorno's dictum that 'The inhumanity of art must triumph over the inhumanity of the world for the sake of the humane.'

That said, one needn't look far to find the ideals covertly driving Timon's tirades overtly adumbrated in the first half of the play. To make his servant Lucilius 'an equal husband' for the rich man's daughter he loves, Timon promises 'To build his fortune' because ''tis a bond in men' (1.1.144, 147–8): in other words, it's a *human* obligation to do so, which matters more than the financial bond it entails. In contrast to Apemantus, who is described in the opening scene as 'opposite to humanity', Timon, we are told, 'outgoes / The very heart of kindness' (1.1.276–8). 'Kindness', as we've seen, is a crucial concept, indeed a fundamental value, for Shakespeare, in whose time the word retained its root sense of showing others the consideration, care and generosity they deserve simply by virtue of belonging to the same kind, the same species, as oneself. ''Tis lack of kindly warmth they are not kind' (2.2.213), says Timon, as the true nature of his fair-weather friends belatedly dawns on him. And as he tears off his clothes, Lear-like, to flee naked from Athens and the life he once knew, he declares: 'Timon will to the woods, where he shall find / Th'unkindest beast more kinder than mankind' (4.1.35–6). The fact that Timon is portrayed from the start as pathologically self-deluded, and arguably motivated in part by a narcissistic infatuation with his selfless image of himself, doesn't invalidate the ideal of gratuitous mutual kindness he repeatedly exemplifies 'But in a dream of friendship' (4.2.34), as his faithful steward Flavius puts it. Even in the mock grace he says, before the mock banquet of hot water and stones he serves his 'smiling, smooth, detested parasites' (3.7.93), Timon asks the gods to 'Lend to each man enough that one need not lend to another' (3.7.73–4); a plea which, notwithstanding its caustic punchline, brings to mind

Gloucester's prayer ending 'So distribution should undo excess / And each man have enough' in *King Lear*, the play with whose mood and vision *Timon of Athens* has so much in common.

The problem is not so much that Timon is a delusional fool, which from a cynical Apemantine standpoint, or from the pragmatic standpoint of his steward, he obviously is. Nor is it that the ideals of human relationship and conduct to which Timon subscribes are misconceived or impossible for human beings to attain. On the contrary: Timon's servants (in a scene mostly scripted by Middleton) enact those ideals in a modest, undemonstrative way, which puts the wealthy elite of Athens to shame: 'Good fellows all,' says the Steward to the rest of Timon's servants, 'All broken implements of a ruined house':

> The latest of my wealth I'll share amongst you.
> Wherever we shall meet, for Timon's sake
> Let's yet be fellows ...
> > *He gives them money*
> > ... Let each take some.
> Nay, put out all your hands. Not one word more.
> Thus part we rich in sorrow, parting poor.
>
> > (4.2.16, 22–9)

The problem, as the play dramatizes it, is not Timon but the time in which he finds himself. The absurdly altruistic Timon is an alien being transported back to Shakespeare's early modern epoch from some imaginary realm in which genuine friendship is a reality, not a dream, and mutual empathy and disinterested generosity based on our common human bond are normal.

Thus when Timon proceeds to think, feel and act as if he and everyone around him already dwelt in that realm, he inevitably looks at worst like an idiot, at best like a holy fool, and his motives are just as inevitably tainted by the suspicion that he's secretly driven by the same egotistical urge to possess and dominate as everyone else. And when Timon wakes from his dream of friendship and realizes how the world really wags, his vitriolic misanthropy and hunger for oblivion are the apt reactions of an immigrant from an ethos so alien to Shakespeare's time and ours that they strike us as inhuman; whereas Timon's inhumanity is in fact the precise measure of the distance that divorces us from the full realization of our positive human potential. Timon's response is the commensurate response of the future to the past, of the way things could and should be to the way they were and are. The Shakespeare who wrote the great misanthropic scenes of *Timon of Athens* would have known exactly what Apollinaire meant when he declared: 'Artists are men who, above all, want to become inhuman.'

Timon of Athens is perhaps best understood as a theatrical thought-experiment, which accounts in part for its abstract, almost allegorical, diagrammatic form; as a *drame à these* designed to pose and answer the questions: What would happen if an incarnation of human kindness, the living embodiment of true community, materialized in our midst, marooned far from home in a still barbaric era? How would he be treated by our world and how would our world look to him? As I'm not the first to notice, there's something distinctly Nietzschean *avant la lettre* about Timon. '*We who are homeless*', Nietzsche writes in *The Gay Science*, 'We children of the future, how *could* we be at home in this today? ... Being new, nameless, hard to understand, we premature births of an as yet unproven future'. Especially with Timon's 'Seek not my name' on his enigmatic epitaph in mind, it's by no means fanciful to regard him as a child of the future, destined to die homeless and misunderstood. Indeed, in its anachronistic incongruity with the age of Shakespeare the whole posthumous play, which was never performed in Shakespeare's day and took centuries to find its audience, may be regarded, like all Shakespeare's plays and poetry rightly understood, as the premature birth of an as yet unproven future.

The need not just to view the present from the virtual vantage point of a more desirable future, but to reveal the possibility of such a future within a reality that seems to preclude it, is at the heart of Shakespeare's creative enterprise, as the most memorable scene in *Timon of Athens* attests. It's the scene in which Timon, having stripped off his rank and identity with his clothes, and having reduced himself to the same poor, bare, forked animal that Lear perceived beneath Poor Tom's rags and his own royal robes, kneels down to dig up a root to eat and digs up the last thing he needs or wants: gold. The word occurs more often in *Timon* (36 times) than in any Shakespeare play, and for good reason: because in this play more than any other, as Marx perceived, Shakespeare 'excellently depicts the real nature of money', the universal leveller that dissolves all distinctions and renders the impossible possible; the deity whose 'divine power ... lies in its *character* as men's estranged, alienating, and self-disposing *species-nature*. Money is the *alienated ability of mankind*.' In other words, in the capitalist economy, both in Shakespeare's time and even more so now, all the needs and capacities of the human species are condensed into an omnipotent abstraction – money – which thereby acquires power over every individual and society as a whole. So in the gold he unearths instead of the roots he needs to eat, Timon beholds nothing less than the supreme symbol of the alienated power of mankind, the source of humanity's dehumanization.

In this extraordinary scene we behold the naked personification of unaccommodated man, the distorted image of pure human potential, confronting the substance that epitomizes the private expropriation of that potential by the capitalist mode of production, to whose now globalized sway we are all in thrall, with consequences so patently catastrophic for most of humanity that it would be otiose to point them out. But, as Timon's subsequent glorification of the visible god shows, the man-made bane of human existence, that 'sold'rest close impossibilities / And mak'st them kiss, that speak'st with every tongue / To every purpose', is also an inverted avatar of the collective human powers from which we have been alienated, and whose reclamation to serve the common interests of the human community rather than the private interests of capital is so imperative today. In the gold can be discerned the negative image of the positive human potential we desperately need to command, which is why Timon's eulogy of gold is not only bitterly ironic, but also rapturously utopian. 'The universal regard for money', as George Bernard Shaw, that dazzling dialectician and self-confessed 'unsocial socialist', once remarked, 'is the one hopeful fact in our civilization.'

Disclosing the potential for revolutionary transformation latent in divisive and oppressive realities by travelling imaginatively forwards in time and adopting a universal human standpoint is a fundamental strategy of Shakespeare's plays and poetry. And, as *Timon of Athens* so uncompromisingly attests, adopting posthumous perspectives on a present which is now our past is one of the most disturbing and resourceful forms that strategy takes.

IV

In *The Final Act of Mr. Shakespeare* Robert Winder portrays the dramatist convincingly as a subversive visionary at heart, forced to repress his contempt for the powerful or veil it in obliquities, and aware that his true audience will be citizens of centuries to come. In the twilight of his career, in conversation with Richard Burbage, Shakespeare reflects on what he and his fellow actors have achieved, but is not consoled by Burbage's reassurance that the plays are bound to endure, because he knows there's more at stake in them than mere endurance. 'Something has happened that we did not intend', says Shakespeare. 'Our plays are more than plays.' They are more than plays, he goes on to say, because 'you and I, Richard, and the others have been writing England's future too. The stories we have told will shape the times to come':

'When I close my eyes,' said Shakespeare, 'I see future generations, crowds of men and women we shall never know. I imagine them crossing a bridge across a flood swollen with strange craft. They walk with their heads down. They are our children's children, and their children too. We cannot know how their lives will be, but their past ... their past is our concern. This is what I believe, Richard: the past they have will be the one we compose. Our version – our drama – this is what they will inherit, believe, even fight for. I would not have them struggle for a lie.'

I think Winder succeeds in capturing here the spirit in which Shakespeare's plays were written. He understands that Shakespeare dramatized the way things were in his time in the knowledge that he was dramatizing what would one day be the past upon which generations to come would look back, and from which, for good or for ill, they would take their bearings.

To put it another way, Shakespeare would have found that fine Irish poet Derek Mahon's belief that 'We live now in a future / Prehistory' immediately intelligible. For his dramatic imagination, as I've endeavoured to demonstrate, perceives the reality of his world as the prospective past of a possible future, which was already incubating within that reality. This future-perfect perspective is succinctly articulated in Diana's words to Bertram as she dupes him into falling for the bed-trick in *All's Well*. After Bertram has given her the ring that will prove his undoing in the dénouement, Helena tells him:

> on your finger in the night I'll put
> Another ring that, what in time proceeds,
> May token to the future our past deeds.

(4.2.62–4)

What makes these lines a paradigm of the frame of mind in which Shakespeare crafts his plays is not just their proleptic point of view, their anticipation of later events, but their speaker's covert understanding – indeed her covert intention – that the future will place a different construction on the past from the one it originally appeared to support.

Faith in the future's capacity to apprehend the full significance of present words or deeds finds figurative expression
elsewhere in the plays that links it to texts and reading. In
Troilus and Cressida, for example, Nestor remarks of the
'wild action' he and Ulysses are plotting:

> for the success,
> Although particular, shall give a scantling
> Of good or bad unto the general –
> And in such indices, although small pricks
> To their subsequent volumes, there is seen
> The baby figure of the giant mass
> Of things to come at large.

(1.3.334–40)

Here the fusion of the metaphor of a printed tome with the
innuendo about the swellings that spring from 'small pricks'
binds books to the gestation and evolution of meaning in
the light of 'subsequent' reading. A similar conceit governs
Volumnia's words to Coriolanus as she presents his son to
him:

> This is a poor epitome of yours,
> Which by th' interpretation of full time
> May show like all yourself.

(5.3.67–9)

Young Martius's embryonic resemblance to his father is
likened to the abridged version or abstract of a complete text;
the full-grown man is legible in the features of the boy. Just
as everything a volume contains is latent in the list of contents
that precedes the text proper, it can also be inferred from
the synopsis that secretes its fully expanded import. In the
quotation from *Coriolanus*, however, the realization of the
text's semantic potential is seen as depending on 'th' interpretation of full time' – on how the text is construed when the
time is ripe for that reading to be revealed. The implication

is that texts may prove to have been so incongruous with their culture that only with the passage of time can their implicit significance become explicitly intelligible to their true contemporaries.

The fact that such complex hermeneutic considerations are woven into the figurative language of the plays suggests how acutely aware of them Shakespeare was, and how readily his mind reached for them. It also illustrates his disconcerting ability to anticipate what his plays demand of any interpretation that attempts to do justice to them today. As a dramatist who dreamt up memories of the future, both the future that for us is now the past and the future that may lie ahead of us, Shakespeare would doubtless have endorsed the White Queen's observation in *Alice in Wonderland* that 'It's a poor sort of memory that only works backwards'. Nor would the author of the English and Roman history plays have had any difficulty grasping what Paul Ricoeur, the doyen of modern hermeneutic philosophy, was driving at, when he stated: 'The promise of an historical event is always more than was actually realised. There is more in the past than what happened. And so we have to find the *future of the past*, the unfulfilled potential of the past.' The historian Dominick LaCapra advocates a similar approach, whose aptitude for unlocking the interpretive potential of Shakespeare's plays is equally apparent. LaCapra rejects the historicist 'rhetoric of contextualization' that has produced, in historical and literary studies alike, far too many 'narrowly documentary readings in which the text becomes little more than a sign of the times'. He rejects it not least because 'historians in an important sense do not know how it all turned out', and he commends instead 'the attempt to explore alternative possibilities in the past that are themselves suggested by the retrospective or deferred effects of later knowledge'.

As far as our reinterpretation of the imaginative literature of the past, especially the remote past, is concerned, it's hard to think of anything more consistently calculated to confound the 'rhetoric of contextualization', and to reward critical inquiries 'into the unrealized or even resisted possibilities of the past' (to quote LaCapra again) than the drama of Shakespeare. Certainly no literature of the past bears out more powerfully Ernst Bloch's contention that

> Every great work of art, above and beyond its manifest content, is carried out according to the latency of the page to come, or in other words, in the light of a future which has not yet come into being, and indeed of some ultimate resolution as yet unknown.

This idea of unfolding alternative futures, which might otherwise remain imprisoned in the past, by allowing Shakespeare's plays to reach forwards to us as we reach back to them, strikes me as especially compelling. To recognize Shakespeare as the untimely author of plays which are the 'premature births of an as yet unproven future', the creations of a dramatist who never felt at home in his today, is to grasp something vital about them that most critical accounts, especially those of an historicist bent, have been blind to, but that it's crucial to grasp in order to understand not only why they still matter after 400 years, but also why they matter today more than ever before.

As *Timon of Athens* makes plain, dwelling imaginatively in the virtual domain of the afterlife afforded Shakespeare far more than a stance of disinterested detachment from his age and his culture – the alleged impartiality for which he has so long, and so mistakenly, been lauded. It opened the horizon of futurity in his plays, allowing them to reveal the possibility of human beings living on radically different terms from those on which they lived in the early modern world and sadly still live, in so many ways, in our world. It enabled Shakespeare 'to preoccupate future things', as Montaigne puts it: to prefigure alternative realities in the course of dramatizing the unendurable tragedies and farcical absurdities that sprang from his world as it was. And, given that he wrote in the expectation of being read by 'eyes not yet created', and of his lines being spoken by 'tongues to be', it empowered him to write in a way that would allow those living 'In states unborn and accents yet unknown', including ourselves, to find in his plays 'the *future of the past*, the unfulfilled potential of the past' that Ricoeur enjoins us to discover now in the literature of long ago.

'And nothing brings me all things': for Shakespeare, the fulfilment of that potential, which Timon could achieve through the annihilation of death alone, implicitly demands that nothing of the existing order of things remain. If 'the possibility of a complete exit from the present order of this life', to which, in Bakhtin's view, the plays attest, is to become a future reality for humanity, then nothing but the abolition of systemic inequality of every kind, and of the unequal distribution of wealth and power that supports it, will suffice. The unfulfilled potential dramatically and poetically articulated in Shakespeare's plays is the potential of all human beings, in his time and in ours, to live on terms authorized by their innate equality and the universal rights that flow from it. Once the true nature and significance of Shakespeare's universality are understood, the 'fine revolution' his drama foreshadows can be seen without any trick at all.

WORKS CITED

All quotations from the plays and poems are from *The Complete Works*, second edition, ed. Stanley Wells, Gary Taylor, John Jowett and William Montgomery (2005). I have, however, retained the First Folio's question marks in preference to the Oxford edition's exclamation marks in the speeches of Cassius and Brutus (*Julius Caesar*, 3.1.112–17) quoted in Chapter 2. I have also restored from the First Folio, for the reason explained in Chapter 4, the first of Timon's three epitaphs ('Timon is dead, who hath outstretched his span. / Some beast read this; there does not live a man.'), which the Oxford edition cuts.

The quotation from Dr Johnson is taken from the 'Preface' (1765) in *Samuel Johnson on Shakespeare*, ed. Woudhuysen (1989). Quotations from Coleridge are from *Coleridge on Shakespeare*, ed. Hawkes (1969). The quotations from Hazlitt can be found in his essay 'On Shakespeare and Milton' (1818) and the chapter on *Measure for Measure* in his *Characters of Shakespear's Plays* (1817). I found Emerson's observation on Shakespeare in John Gross's anthology *After Shakespeare* (2002). The quotation from Apollinaire can be found in *Oeuvres en prose complètes: Tome II*, ed. Cazergues and Décaudin (1991; my translation). For the quotations from Chesterton see his essays on *King Lear* and *A Midsummer Night's Dream* in *The Soul of Wit: G. K. Chesterton on William Shakespeare*, ed. Ahlquist (2012). The quotation from Shaw can be found in his 'Preface to *Major Barbara*' (1906) and the quotations from Middleton Murry in his study *Shakespeare* (1936).

The quotation from Adorno in Chapter 3 can be found in *Minima Moralia*, trans. Jephcott (1974) and the aphorism cited in Chapter 4 in *Philosophy of Modern Music*, trans. Mitchell and Blomster (2004). The quotation from Bloch in Chapter 2 is from *The Utopian Function of Art and Literature: Selected Essays*, trans. and ed. Zipes and Mecklenberg (1988); the one in Chapter 4 can be found in Fredric Jameson's *Marxism and Form* (1971; Jameson's translation). The quotations from Bakhtin in Chapter 3 are from *Speech Genres and Other Late Essays*, trans. and ed. Emerson and Holquist (1986), and *The Dialogic Imagination*, trans. and ed. Emerson and Holquist (1981), while the one in Chapter 4 is from *Rabelais and his World*, trans. Iswolsky (1968). *After Babel* (1975) is the source of the quotation from George Steiner. The quotations from Dominick LaCapra are taken from *Rethinking Intellectual History* (1983). The book by David Scott Kastan quoted in the opening chapter is *Shakespeare after Theory* (1999). The quotation from Ricoeur can be found in 'Paul Ricoeur: On Narrative Imagination', in *Debates in Continental Philosophy*, ed. Kearney (2004). The quotation from Fredric Jameson comes from his essay 'Symptoms of Theory or Symptoms for Theory' in *Critical Inquiry*, 30 (2004). A. D. Nuttall's characterization of *Timon* crops up in *Shakespeare the Thinker* (2007). And Nadine Gordimer's remarks on writing posthumously appear in 'Nadine Gordimer Interview by Ting Chang', *Scrivener Creative Review* (Winter, 1984) and 'An Interview with Nadine Gordimer', *Virginia Quarterly Review*, 3 December 2007.

INDEX

Ambiguous, Shakespeare can be interpreted in so many different ways, His characters can be portrayed in different ways.